MONASTIC WISDOM SERIES: NUMBER TWENTY-EIGHT

I Am the Way

MONASTIC WISDOM SERIES: NUMBER TWENTY-EIGHT

I Am the Way

Stages of Prayer in Saint Bernard

Maureen F. McCabe, OCSO

Foreword by John Sommerfeldt

Cistercian Publications
www.cistercianpublications.org

LITURGICAL PRESS
Collegeville, Minnesota
www.litpress.org

A Cistercian Publications title published by Liturgical Press

Cistercian Publications
Editorial Offices
Abbey of Gethsemani
3642 Monks Road
Trappist, Kentucky 40051
www.cistercianpublications.org

1 2 3 4 5 6 7 8 9

Library of Congress Cataloging-in-Publication Data

McCabe, Maureen F.
I am the way : stages of prayer in Saint Bernard / Maureen F. McCabe.
p. cm. — (Monastic wisdom series ; no. 28)
ISBN 978-0-87907-028-1 — ISBN 978-0-87907-476-0 (e-book)
1. Bernard, of Clairvaux, Saint, 1090 or 91-1153. 2. Contemplation.
I. Title.

BV5091.C7M37 2012
248.2—dc23 2011041792

For the Cistercian Friends
of Mt. Saint Mary's Abbey, Wrentham,
who have taught me so much
about prayer and love

Contents

Foreword

As we learn by experience how much we need the spirituality of others, we seek out those who can aid us in our journey to God. Mother Maureen has illuminated the path by relating the riches gained through her own experience, an experience enriched by her sensitive reading of Saint Bernard the spiritual guide.

Often in my many travels to the monasteries of America and Europe I have heard my monastic sisters and brothers express their discomfort in reading Bernard. His thought, they say, is too difficult to relate to "my real, everyday life." They are right: Bernard is indeed difficult.

A large part of our difficulty in understanding Bernard is due to the many myths which have grown up about him. The first myth is that Bernard condemned his brilliant contemporary Peter Abelard for attempting to apply reason or logic to matters of faith. But Bernard's complaint was that Abelard had applied logic to questions beyond logic—like the doctrine of the Blessed Trinity—and that that application of logic was . . . illogical. Bernard gave the church deep insights into her doctrine, most often by the logical analysis of Scripture.

A related myth is that Bernard believed that the only certain way to knowing the truth about God, humankind, and nature was through contemplation—a direct experience of the reality of God. Bernard was indeed a contemplative and urged his brother monks and all of us to be open to God's gift of contemplative experience. But he also subscribed to other means of knowing the truth: the certainty attained by faith, for instance, and the charismatic knowledge imparted directly to the mind as a gift of the

Holy Spirit. Bernard also showed himself a humanist who saw beauty, especially the beauty of language, as an effective way of experiencing and sharing the reality of God and his world. Perhaps more surprising, Bernard also believed that philosophy too could lead to truth and the Truth who is God.

A third Bernardine myth is that our saint ignored the world of nature as a distraction from spiritual pursuits. Not at all! The universe in which Bernard dwelled was energized, he was sure, by the creating and redeeming power of love, the love of a Creator God who is Love. All of creation, both material and spiritual, is immersed in the sea of God's overwhelming goodness and indwelling love.

Contrary to still another myth about him, Bernard did not believe that humans were totally incapacitated by original sin. The truth is that Bernard was convinced that human beings, though flawed by self-centeredness, are basically good because God created them good. He saw them capable of the happiness for which they all long and for which God destines them. And for Bernard the body is so essential to human nature and its perfection that we cannot fully enjoy the beatitude of heaven until our souls are reunited with our bodies, glorified at the end of time.

Yet another myth is that Bernard followed Saint Augustine's views in all things. Bernard did depend greatly on Augustine's thought, but he differed radically on some questions of great importance to us. Augustine, for instance, saw the human soul as having three principal powers: the intellect for knowing, the will for choosing, and the memory for remembering. But, for memory in the Augustinian scheme, Bernard substituted a wholly different power: the *affectus,* which functions in human attachment, emotion, feeling, and passion. Passion he did not reject as evil, and Augustine's aversion to sex he rejected out of hand. We all know of Bernard's *Sermons on the Song of Songs,* in which, over a period of some eighteen years, he lyrically portrayed the union of human lovers as a convincing symbol of Christ's passionate love for each and every human being.

Bernard did not believe, as has been stated even in recent books, that the monastic life was by far the highest vocation. Rather, he saw each person and every vocation having a place and a role in a process very much like a pilgrimage. That pilgrimage has as its goal individual fulfillment and the perfection of the whole People of God.

It has taken me nearly seventy years of study even to begin to understand the richness of Bernard's teaching on the spiritual life. Mother Maureen has helped you and me as her readers to profit, virtually without effort, from following Bernard's prayerful path to God.

Surely there is no better way to learn how to pray more deeply than to consult a guide whose prayer life is already profound. Mother Maureen has enriched her prayer life by listening to Saint Bernard. In the same way, we who long to pray more profoundly are able, through this book, to listen to one whose prayer life mirrors Bernard's and has brought her before the face of God.

I believe introductions should be short. This is especially true of this book. I do not want to delay your feasting on its riches.

John Sommerfeldt, PhD
University of Dallas

Abbreviations

CF	Cistercian Fathers Series
CS	Cistercian Studies Series
Conv	Bernard, *Sermons to Clerics on Conversion*
Csi	Bernard, *Five Books on Consideration*
Dil	Bernard, *On the Love of God* (*De diligendo Deo*)
Hum	Bernard, *On the Steps of Humility and Pride*
Pre	Bernard, *On Precept and Dispensation*
QH	Bernard, *Lenten Sermons on the Psalm "He Who Dwells"* (*Qui habitat*)
RB	Rule of Saint Benedict
SC	Bernard, *Sermons on the Song of Songs* (*Super Cantica*)
Sent	Bernard, *The Parables and the Sentences*

We have here three stages of the soul's growth in love,
three stages of its advance toward perfection
that are sufficiently known and intelligible
to those who have experienced them.
There is first the forgiveness of sins,
then the grace that follows on good deeds,
and finally
that contemplative gift by which a kind and beneficent Lord
shows himself to the soul
with as much clarity as bodily frailty can endure.[1]

1. *Sermons on the Song of Songs*, CF 4 (Kalamazoo, MI: Cistercian Publications, 1971), 22.

Introduction: The Journey

From one point of view it is presumptuous, and even preposterous, that I should write a book about Saint Bernard; yet from another nothing could be more natural. I have the joy of accompanying Cistercian laypersons on their spiritual journey, persons with a great hunger for and fidelity to prayer. And when it comes to my own prayer, what can I say? Simply that, after God, it was Saint Bernard who taught me how to pray, who has accompanied me my entire Cistercian journey, and whose guidance I have tried to share with our group of lay associates at Wrentham. As a result I have been strongly encouraged to share the same with others on their spiritual journey.

This is why in this modest book I have endeavored above all to allow Bernard's voice to be heard, in all its resonance and penetration, and so at times I have refrained from giving any commentary on certain lengthy texts of his that speak for themselves. I am happy if I have thus provided the reader with a kind of anthology of Bernardine texts that have affected me the most.

Born near Dijon in 1090, Bernard entered Cîteaux in its early years, receiving there a formation in Cistercian spirituality that he later articulated in writings of great power, beauty, and depth. As founding abbot of Clairvaux, his extraordinary giftedness and good judgment were often called upon by church and secular powers, and in that realm his profound interior freedom, persuasiveness, conviction, and joy were either the delight or the dismay of those who encountered him.

But when it comes to prayer, Bernard can only delight. Anyone who gives him a chance will discover teachings full of unction and spiritual discernment. He draws us to continual prayer through a continual confidence in the One who believes in our capacity to love without limits no matter what state we're in or what stage we're at, and this through continual gratitude for and reflection upon the mercies of the Lord, especially in his passion. Bernard is truly a father—father of the church and father of souls.

The *journey* is a universal image for human life and, in the Judæo-Christian tradition, a classic image for growth in prayer, expressing as it does a profound interior reality: the heart's search for its true homeland.

> O Lord, you have always been our home. (Ps 90:1; TEV)
>
> This will be a returning home: to have left the land of the body for the region of the spirit, which is our God.[1]

Even a little taste of home can be enough to set our feet in the right direction, and Bernard is lavish with images describing those tastes, those moments of arrival, be they ever so brief and rare during our earthly life. They are an embrace,[2] a kiss,[3] a sense of being held from within;[4] they are like a drop of water which disappears completely in wine,[5] or like silence in heaven for half an hour;[6] they are the length, the width, the height, and the depth of God making God's way into our experience;[7] and they are a walk in the "hidden home of truth itself"[8]—to name but a few of Bernard's images. One particularly beautiful image is used by Wil-

1. *Five Books on Consideration*, CF 37 (Kalamazoo, MI: Cistercian Publications, 1976), 141.

2. *SC*, CF 40 (Kalamazoo, MI: Cistercian Publications, 1980), 182, 186; CF 7 (Kalamazoo, MI: Cistercian Publications, 1976), 96.

3. See *SC*, CF 4:47–52.

4. *SC*, CF 7:129.

5. See *Liber de diligendo Deo, Treatises II*, CF 13B (Washington, DC: Cistercian Publications, 1974), 120.

6. See *Liber de gradibus humilitatis et superbiæ, Treatises II*, CF 13A (Washington, DC: Cistercian Publications, 1974), 50.

7. *Csi*, CF 37:175.

8. *Hum*, CF 13A:53.

liam of Saint Thierry to describe Bernard's motivation for entering Cîteaux: the yearning to be hidden in the hiding place of God's face.[9]

It is the journey's end which sets the beginning in motion, and once in motion every journey has its delights and difficulties, its stages and milestones. Bernard works carefully, though not systematically, with these aspects of journeying, sometimes mingling this imagery with that of the ladder, sometimes with that of the mountain, both of which give the sense of a climb, often arduous. But the most striking Bernardine trait in the journey theme is *Jesus the Way*:

> Imitate him and you will not walk in darkness but will have the light of life. What is the light of life but truth that enlightens every man that comes into this world and shows us where the true life is to be found? So when he says: "I am the Way and the Truth," he adds "and the Life." It is as if he said: "I am the Way, I lead to Truth; I am the Truth, I promise Life; and I am myself the very Life I give you" . . . But what if the way is so difficult that I can never reach the goal? The answer comes promptly: "I am the Life, that is, I am the food, the viaticum, to sustain you on your journey.[10]

Bernard has cleared a path for us, a prayer path, and because his spirit is so profoundly Cistercian we may truly call it a Cistercian prayer path. Let us go with him because he calls to us as he once called to his own brothers in his early years at Clairvaux:

> Already I see God, resting on the top of the ladder; already I have the joy of hearing the voice of Truth. He calls to me and I reply to him: "Stretch out your right hand to the work of your hands." You have numbered my steps, O Lord, but I am a slow climber, a weary traveler, and I need a resting place. Woe is me if darkness should overtake me, or if my flight should be in

9. William of Saint Thierry, *Bernard of Clairvaux* (Guadalupe Translations, 1989), 1:13.

10. *Hum*, CF 13A:29–30.

winter or on the Sabbath seeing that now, in an acceptable time, on the day of salvation, I can hardly grope my way to the light. Why am I so slow? O, if any is to me a son, a brother in the Lord, a comrade, one who shares my journey, let him pray for me![11]

11. *Hum,* CF 13A:53.

Stage One

*To you, Lord Jesus, how truly my
heart has said: "My face looks to
you. Lord, I do seek your face."
In the dawn you brought me proof
of your love; in my first approach
to kiss your revered feet you forgave
my evil ways as I lay in the dust.*[1]

1. *SC*, CF 4:20

1

The Return to the Heart

For Bernard the first step of the journey home is inward, the return to the heart, and in that return we travel by stages. Bernard is both flexible and creative in describing various sets of "stages"—three levels of truth, four degrees of love, seven infusions of the Holy Spirit, and so on—and, while capturing multiple nuances in his various descriptions, he offers enough common elements for each stage that we cannot miss the path. In addition, all of these stages in Bernard are enfolded within two that bring us to the very heart of his thought on prayer:

> I think this is the principal reason why the invisible God willed to be seen in the flesh and to converse with men as a man. He wanted to recapture the affections of carnal men who were unable to love in any other way, by first drawing them to the salutary love of his own humanity, and then gradually to raise them to a spiritual love.[1]

Here we have two immensely beautiful ways of loving God, of relating to him—in short, of praying; two stages of prayer that respect both human development and human weakness, the second building on the first; two ways that reveal that the very heart of Bernard's prayer path is Jesus Christ. As far as content goes, these two ways of praying are at the very heart of my study; as

1. *SC*, CF 4:152.

far as structure is concerned, I will work with the classic division of the three stages that Bernard uses: the beginners, the proficient, and the perfect. At the beginning of Part II, however, I will introduce Bernard's thoughts on the seven infusions of the Holy Spirit as a means of considering the second and third stages in greater depth and detail.

But before we look more closely at the stages through which we pass as we travel inward, it is important to ask where we are when we are not in our heart. Where are we but *outside* it? We are, as Bernard loved to describe it, walking around in circles outside ourselves, caught on the surface, superficial and peripheral.[2] Or, in an image he used even more frequently, we are *below* ourselves like the beasts that perish for lack of knowledge.[3]

What brings about this sad condition? Bernard names several significant factors, the first of which is natural, at least natural for wounded human nature: "Since nature has become more fragile and weak, necessity obliges man to serve it first. This is carnal love by which a man loves himself above all for his own sake. He is only aware of himself; as Saint Paul says: 'What was animal came first, then what is spiritual.'"[4] *He is only aware of himself.* This all-absorbing preoccupation should, however, lead to awareness of the other, for sooner or later one discovers—or has it brought forcibly to one's attention—that a "neighbor has the same rights" as oneself.[5]

Our hearts rejoice to see sensitivity to others, and ultimately to the Other, unfolding in children; but, from the experience of our deep-seated inclination to be primarily aware of our own needs, preferences, and well-being, we all know what a long journey lies ahead for this sensitivity to become an abiding disposition. Our

2. See *Dil*, CF 13B:112; *Lenten Sermons on the Psalm "He Who Dwells,"* CF 25 (Kalamazoo, MI: Cistercian Publications, 1981), 213–14.

3. See Bernard's frequent use of Psalm 49 to illustrate this theme; see, for example, *QH*, CF 25:129, 153; *SC*, CF 40:172.

4. *Dil*, CF 13B:115.

5. *Dil*, CF 13B:116.

excessive self-awareness, not to be confused with the interiority of self-knowledge, is also exacerbated by other factors.

A primary one is the healthy restlessness natural to desire, which, when it foolishly rejects what would lead it to its true end ("which is not in consumption but in consummation"[6]), gets caught up in multiple desires: "When will they reach him whom they do not want to reach until they have tested all the rest? The desire to experience all things first is like a vicious circle, it goes on forever."[7] Another significant factor is unreal comfort, that is, the turning of one's whole attention to one side so that one may put away all thought of sorrow and remain always merry, the cutting out of the mind of all discreditable and, therefore, distressing recollections.[8] Then there is curiosity, which reveals itself as sluggishness in self-examination but inquisitiveness about others, a tendency to dwell on the shortcomings of one's neighbor without sufficient attention to one's own.[9]

Finally comes a factor which seems to be the ultimate degree of unreal comfort: a numbness brought about by inner insensitivity. The mind isn't at home and the soul feels her wounds so little that she has forgotten who she is, being inwardly estranged from herself. She has taken a journey into a far country. Dead from the heart, she is unacquainted with herself.[10] At this point it is clear that one is far, very far, from home.

Each person is located somewhere on this continuum of inner insensitivity. Each needs some way, something, someone to pierce through her coarseness, to puncture her hardness, and it is here that we meet the precise meaning of *compunction*, a word Bernard and others use often in describing the beginnings of prayer. Compunction (from *pungo*, "to pierce") is that experience of God that arouses the dull mind and urges the self-absorbed heart to take

6. *Dil*, CF 13B:112.
7. *Dil*, CF 13B:113.
8. See *Hum*, CF 13A:67.
9. See *Hum*, CF 13A:57.
10. See *Sermones ad clericos de conversione*, CF 25 (Kalamazoo, MI: Cistercian Publications, 1981), 37–38.

the path that extends from outside to inside, from circumference to center, from the far country to home. Compunction is the way to return to our heart.

It is not necessary for you to cross the seas,
nor to pierce the clouds, nor to climb mountains
to meet your God.
It is not a lengthy road that is set before you;
you have only to enter into yourself to find him.
"For his word is very near you;
it is on your lips and in your heart."
Encounter him in compunction of heart
and in confession of your sins.[11]

11. *Sermo in adventu Domini, A Word in Season*, Vol. 1, Advent–Christmastide (Dublin: The Talbot Press, 1973), 24.

2

Pain Punctures: *Miseria/Compunctio*

If anything has power to puncture the illusion of well-being in our lives and to open us to deeper possibilities, to a deep heart,[1] it is misery. We all know that pain has its blessings both in revealing that we are sick and in propelling us to health.

Saint Bernard has a profound and practical sense of the place of misery in our prayer life and he speaks of it frequently. In *Sermon 12* on the Song of Songs he even gives us a "collection of manifold miseries": the needs of the poor, the anxieties of the oppressed, the worries of those who are sad, the sins of wrong-doers, the manifold misfortunes of people of all classes.[2] These miseries, common to all of us at some time or another, are not punishments but, as Bernard puts it, tribulations God permits so that, in turning to him for help, we may experience his mercy—*miseria* meets *misericordia*—and so that in that experience, frequently renewed, we may begin to know and love God for himself. "Man's frequent needs oblige him to invoke God more often and approach him more frequently. This intimacy moves man to taste and discover how sweet the Lord is. Tasting God's sweetness entices us more to pure love than does the urgency of our own needs."[3]

1. *Hum,* CF 13A:43.
2. See *SC,* CF 4:77.
3. *Dil,* CF 13B:117–18; see also *SC,* CF 7:179.

When we are granted these moments of intimacy, a fire stirs within us and we are prompted to give ourselves more seriously and frequently to prayer. We may even feel a sense of urgency to pray always and to live in an abiding attentiveness to God's voice within. When this happened to me I quickly discovered that such dedication brings with it its own peculiar experience of misery, unprepared as I was to face how undeveloped my capacity for prayer really was and how much I interiorly resisted this gift. Frequently I would be reminded of the contrast between myself and Saint Bernard as I passed his statue on the stairway that led to my room (a statue that looked more like a particular American abbot than any likeness I had ever seen of Bernard!). One day I asked him point-blank why he had been such a fervent novice while I was such a poor one. He didn't take long to answer. Without my asking, my novice director gave me Bernard's *Sermons on the Song of Songs,* which contains his own description of his first attempts at prayer. This passage has ever since brought me relief and encouragement, first of all because I could identify so completely with what it says, and secondly because Bernard here gives such sound reasons for God's wisdom in permitting this initial difficulty:

> I am not ashamed to admit that very often I myself, especially in the early days of my conversion, experienced coldness and hardness of heart, while deep in my being I sought for him whom I longed to love. I could not love him since I had not really found him; at best my love was less than it should have been, and for that reason I sought to increase it, for I would not have sought him if I did not already love him in some degree. I sought him therefore that in him my numbed and languid spirit might find warmth and repose, for nowhere could I find a friend to help me, whose love would thaw the wintry cold that chilled my inward being, and bring back again the feeling of spring-like bliss and spiritual delight. But my languor and weariness only increased, my soul melted away for sorrow, even to the verge of despair. All I could do was repeat softly to myself: "Who can stand before his cold?" Then, at times when I least expected it, at the word or even the sight of a good and holy

> man, at the memory of a dead or absent friend, he set his wind blowing and the waters flowing, and my tears were my food day and night. How can I explain this? Only by ascribing it to the odor from the oil that anointed the friend in question. For me there was no anointing, but rather the experience that came by another's mediation. And so, though made happy by this favor, I was also embarrassed and humiliated: it was a mere puff of perfumed air, not the dewy sprinkling for which I longed. Given only the pleasure of its odor and not of its touch, I saw myself unworthy of him to whom God himself would communicate his sweetest joys. And even now, if a similar experience should happen to me, I eagerly grasp at the proffered gift, I am grateful for it, even though I feel sad beyond words that I have not won it by my own merits, that despite my urgent request it has not passed directly from his hand to mine. I feel ashamed that the remembrance of human goodness should affect me more powerfully than the thought of God. In these straits I cry out with a groan: "When shall I come and behold the face of God?" Many of you, too, I feel, have had similar experiences, and have them even still. In what light then must we view them? I hold that through them our pride is shown up, our humility guarded, brotherly love fostered and good desires aroused.[4]

His message is clear: persevere through the pain of interior poverty, through the hardness and coldness we meet in our hearts. We are not actually going backward; rather, we are learning by experience how much we need others spiritually, both to rekindle our longing for God by revealing to us his beauty and to make us keenly aware of how far we must travel to reach such depths. Then our experience can become a direct path to humble self-knowledge, which is so much a part of compunction and which is surely not the work of a day.

These depths toward which we journey are actually more natural to us who are made in the image and likeness of God than surface living, for the Spirit who leads us into them "leads us on

4. *SC*, CF 4:102–3.

the way by which we discover ourselves."[5] As Bernard describes it, compunction opens us to secret places within, where we experience a dawning light:

> The first step for the wretched man [*misero*] extricating himself from the depths of vice is the mercy [*misericordia*] which makes him to be merciful [*miseretur*] to the son of his mother, to be merciful [*miseretur*] to his soul, and thereby pleasing to God. In this way he emulates the great work of divine pity [*miserationis*], being moved to tears with him who was pierced for him [*compunctus cum eo, qui prior pro eo punctus est*], somehow dying for his own salvation, and sparing himself no longer. This first act of pity [*miseratio*] sustains the person returning to his heart, and enables him to enter the secret places of his being. . . . Turned back to his heart, he must become little in his own eyes. . . . May he not be ashamed to bring into the light of truth what he cannot see in secret without being moved to pity [*miserationis*].[6]

Here, clearly at the very beginning of the journey, there is a meeting of mercy and truth initiated by the mercy which recognizes our misery not as a curse but as a blessing that beckons us to our interior, true self and urges us to enter into our pain rather than evade it. By so doing we touch in some mysterious way the very pain of Christ who thirsted for our salvation. Our misery meets his misery, and through this shared experience we begin a step-by-step journey into an ever-deepening experience, moving from Jesus in earthly lowliness to moments of Jesus in heavenly beauty—and back again. Let us follow Bernard in his reflection upon four words of Scripture spoken by or about Jesus that are significant in his teaching on prayer in its wonderful and terrible beginnings. These words constitute a summary of what has been traditionally called the *purgative way*:

1. "You are the fairest of the children of men." (Ps 44:3 [45:2]; Grail, 1963)

5. *SC*, CF 4:132.
6. *QH*, CF 25:209–210.

2. "For we do not have a high priest who is unable to sympathize with our weaknesses, but we have one who in every respect has been tested as we are." (Heb 4:15)

3. "I am . . . the truth." (John 14:6)

4. "She stood behind him at his feet, weeping, and began to bathe his feet with her tears and to dry them with her hair. Then she continued kissing his feet and anointing them with the ointment." (Luke 7:38)

It is good for me to be troubled, Lord, as long as you are with me, better than reigning without you, feasting without you, being glorified without you. It is good for me to embrace you in tribulation, to have you with me in the furnace, better than being without you even in heaven. "For whom have I in heaven but you? And there is nothing on earth that I desire beside you." The furnace tests gold, and the trial of tribulation just men. There, yes, there you are present with them, Lord. . . . Why should we tremble, why should we hesitate, why flee this furnace? The fire rages, but the Lord is with us in tribulation. "If God is with us who can be against us?"[7]

7. QH, CF 25:257–58.

3

Jesus, One of Us

"You are the fairest of the children of men." (Ps 44:3 [45:2]; Grail, 1963)

"For we do not have a high priest who is unable to sympathize with our weaknesses, but we have one who in every respect has been tested as we are." (Heb 4:15)

It is appropriate to consider these two verses together because, together, they express the two characteristics of Jesus that are the special grace for our halting beginnings in prayer: his human attractiveness and his humble approachability. He came to meet us where we were, and where were we but in weakness? To recapture our hearts, which had developed little in interiority, he became flesh, not yet glorified flesh, but earthly, lowly, vulnerable flesh. And in this flesh he drew us to his blessed presence in two ways: first, by becoming the most beautiful of the children of men; second, by revealing to us—through his life's sorrows, temptations, and sufferings, culminating in the passion—how much he understands from the inside what we go through, how much sympathy he has for our weakness, and, consequently, how much confidence we should have in approaching the throne of grace through him.

In regard to the first point, Jesus' human attractiveness, Saint Bernard expresses the reason for this with incredible clarity and unction more than once. Here are words from an Ascension sermon:

> Because the disciples were beings of flesh and God is spirit, and spirit and flesh are not easily brought together, he adapted himself to them with the shadow of his body, that by the intervention of his life-giving flesh they might behold the Word in flesh, the sun in a cloud, light in an earthen jug, the candle in the lantern. . . . For this purpose the Lord set his flesh before them, to turn their every thought away from human matters and attach it to his flesh, which was saying wondrous things and performing wondrous deeds.[1]

It is difficult to find a translation that fully conveys the power of this message. In this connection, a reflection from Corneille Halflants in his introduction to Bernard's *Sermons on the Song of Songs* is very helpful:

> Saint Bernard does not believe it possible to suppress with impunity the indestructible force of sense love. On the other hand, it would be illusory to believe that even with the help of grace one could quickly succeed in changing carnal love to spiritual love. What is to be done? Present to carnal love an object which is proportionate to it and more delightful than any sinful creature. Had not Saint Augustine already spoken of the *bona delectio victrix*? Thus Bernard writes: "Your affection for your Lord Jesus should be both tender and intimate, to oppose the sweet enticements of sensual life. Sweetness conquers sweetness as one nail drives out another." Here is the advantage of attaching one's sense love to the humanity of Christ. It directs the vital strength of such love toward a more attractive sensible object. This new sensible object is the dwelling place of the divinity, which will gradually reveal itself as it draws the soul into its holiness.[2]

The way I would explain it from my own experience is this: Bernard had a tremendous respect for *eros* and its power in the spiritual life and prayer. He knew that in a younger person it would be unintegrated *eros*, often raw passion. That was inevitable. So

1. *Sermo in ascensione Domini*, in *Sermons for the Summer Season*, CF 53 (Kalamazoo, MI: Cistercian Publications, 1991), 38–39.
2. *SC*, CF 4:xix–xx.

he seeks tirelessly for a way to channel this precious energy without losing a drop of it, and he found that way—by turning the human heart and all its longings toward the greatest beauty that ever touched our poor earth: the beauty of Jesus, which can captivate the human heart as no other human beauty. The power of this approach is especially evident when one is struggling with a love that seems to be swallowing up one's love of God. It was in one of these moments years ago, a time when I felt my being would break in two, that God sounded an urgent and clear call to freedom in my soul: "*Never* love anyone less; just love me more." Yes, that is the secret: not to deny or squash or kill a love—as if one could—but to recognize and affirm it for what it is worth, because it is worth a great deal, and then to turn the eyes of one's heart gently, surely, persistently toward the Lord. These may be only little steps, but they make all the difference, because if we have turned toward him we will be present for that moment when he takes a giant step toward us, and in so doing, he will set all our loves in order without destroying any of them.

But how do we come to experience this earthly beauty of Jesus in our own time and place? Bernard leads us straight to the Gospels and teaches us to pray with them deeply and frequently:

> Notice that the love of the heart is, in a certain sense, carnal because our hearts are attracted most toward the humanity of Christ and the things he did or commanded while in the flesh. The heart that is filled with this love is quickly touched by every word on this subject. Nothing else is as pleasant to listen to, or is read with as much interest, nothing is as frequently in remembrance or as sweet in reflection. . . . The soul at prayer should have before it a sacred image of the God-man in his birth or infancy or as he was teaching or dying, rising or ascending.[3]

I will return shortly to this very important way of prayer: pondering the Gospels.

3. *SC*, CF 4:152.

The second way Jesus draws us to himself is by making himself humbly accessible to our experience of weakness and, therefore, ever so approachable. This is the point not only of Hebrews 4:15 but of a cluster of texts from Hebrews that Bernard turns to frequently:

1. "Therefore he had to become like his brothers and sisters in every respect, so that he might be a merciful and faithful high priest." (Heb 2:17)
2. "Because he himself was tested by what he suffered, he is able to help those who are being tested." (Heb 2:18)
3. "For we do not have a high priest who is unable to sympathize with our weaknesses." (Heb 4:15)
4. "He is able to deal gently with the ignorant and wayward, since he himself is subject to weakness." (Heb 5:2)

In the spirit of these texts Bernard describes with great eloquence and power the plan God conceived for us in Christ. Our Father, watching us tenderly from afar, observes how difficult the journey is for us, how slow and fearful we are, even to the point of walking in the wrong direction. In his great mercy he comes "forth from his shady and thickly covered mountain" to meet us in Christ,[4] and he meets us just where we are. He doesn't need us to be more advanced. Here in this very first stage he pierces our insensitivity with the most powerful instrument of all: Jesus in human weakness and lowliness:

> I do not see what better meaning you can draw from these words than that being like his brethren in all things means that he willed to suffer and be tempted and share in all human miseries except sin so that, having thus suffered and been tempted, he might learn by experience the lesson of sympathy and mercy. I do not say that he became wiser by such experience, but he was seen as closer to men. And the frail sons of Adam, to whom

4. *SC*, CF 4:33.

> he was willing to give the title and the reality of brothers, would have less hesitation about laying their weaknesses before him, who as God could heal them, as one close would heal them, and as one who had suffered the same would understand. For this reason Isaiah calls him a "man of sorrows and acquainted with infirmity," and the Apostle tells us: "We have not a High Priest who is unable to sympathize with our weakness." Then to show from where this arises, he adds: "One who in every respect has been tempted as we are, but without sinning." The blessed God, the blessed Son of God, in that form in which he did not think it robbery to be equal with the Father, was without doubt impassible before he emptied himself, taking on the form of a slave. Thus he had no experience of misery and subjection, he did not know by experience mercy and obedience. He knew by the knowledge natural to him, but not by experience. He assumed a state that was not only less than what is his by right, but even a little less than that of the angels; for they too are impassible, but by grace, not by nature. Lower still he came to take our form in which he could do what he could not do before: suffer and be subject to authority and learn by experience the mercy of a fellow-sufferer and the obedience of a fellow-subject. As I said already, he did not increase his personal knowledge but he deepened our trust in him when we see him from whom we strayed draw near to us to know our misery by a shared experience. Hardly could we have dared to approach him in his eternal tranquility, but now the Apostle can urge us to go with confidence to the throne of grace because, as he tells us in another place, he has borne our weakness and sorrows and will have compassion on us since he has borne the like.[5]

Again, it is through pondering the Gospels that we open ourselves to this grace of prayer, for of all the moments of his earthly existence that we should ponder, Jesus' sufferings, especially those of his passion, have a unique power to pierce our hearts and draw them to his own. In this prayer journey we begin by being pierced with our own pain, which in turn makes us aware of others' pain. Now, at the peak of compunction, we behold Jesus' pain, a pain

5. *Hum*, CF 13A:37–38.

that can cut us to the quick and lead us to the sorrow that gives life. This will happen when we give our memory over to all that the Gospels reveal to us of his immense and sacrificial love:

> You, too, if you are wise will imitate the prudence of the bride, and never permit even for an hour that this precious bunch of myrrh should be removed from your bosom. Preserve without fail the memory of all those bitter things he endured for you, persevere in meditating on him. . . . As for me, dear Brothers, from the early days of my conversion, conscious of my grave lack of merits, I made sure to gather for myself this little bunch of myrrh and place it between my breasts. It was culled from all the anxious hours and bitter experiences of my Lord; first from the privations of his infancy, then from the hardships he endured in preaching, the fatigues of his journeys, the long watches in prayer, the temptations when he fasted, his tears of compassion, the heckling when he addressed the people, and finally the spitting, the blows, the mockery, the scorn, the nails and similar torments that are multiplied in the Gospels, like trees in the forest, and all for the salvation of our race.[6]

If the first lesson I learned in Bernard's teaching on prayer was to turn to God in my misery rather than to false and numbing securities, the second was to preserve without fail the memory of all he did for us, of all he is for us. This is the way not only of *lectio divina*, prayerful reading, but most particularly of *meditatio*, that is, the pondering of God's words throughout the day, "never permitting even for an hour" that they be far from us. To foster this we must first be faithful, along with Bernard, in returning "day by day to draw waters from the open streams of the Scriptures," so that we may have at hand "spiritual waters for every occasion."[7] Secondly, we must begin to embrace these occasions, that is, the events of a day, every day, with greater consciousness, knowing that in them a continual conversation with the Lord Jesus has the possibility of opening up, for he himself approaches

6. *SC*, CF 7:221–22.
7. *SC*, CF 7:15.

us as he did the disciples on the way to Emmaus to reveal to us the inner meaning of his deeds and words as well as all the words of Scripture that speak of him or point to him. In so doing we must always cherish the centrality of the Gospels.[8] This conversation in turn sheds light on the events of our own lives, moment by moment.

We are not speaking here of psychic tension but of relationship, a relationship that begins right where we are. A surgeon in our lay group is regularly interrupted by his beeper during our meetings and sometimes he must leave to tend to a patient. But for him this isn't really an interruption. He shared with us once that, when he hears his beeper go off, the words that come to mind are "the love of Christ urges me." He shared also something of his experience each day in the hospital, how filled it is with those moments when he is crying out straight from his heart: "O God, come to my assistance. Lord, make haste to help me." This is exactly what is meant to develop in our prayer life, this and much more—a wonderful, ongoing conversation with the one who wishes to be with us in all our joys and sorrows and needs, and with whom we can identify no matter what we go through. Happy the person "who has the Word for an inseparable companion who is always accessible, whose delightful conversation is an unceasing pleasure."[9]

I began these reflections by saying that Jesus draws us to himself by both his human attractiveness and his humble approachability, but these two aspects are so close that they may even be seen as one. As Bernard prays:

> How beautiful you appear to the angels, Lord Jesus, in the form of God, eternal, begotten before the daystar amid the splendors of heaven, "the radiant light of God's glory and the perfect copy of his nature," the unchanging and untarnished brightness of eternal life! How beautiful you are to me, my Lord, even in the

8. See *Dei Verbum*, in *The Documents of Vatican II*, ed. Walter M. Abbott, SJ (New York: Guild Press, 1966), 122.
9. *SC*, CF 7:140.

> very discarding of your beauty! When you divested yourself of the native radiance of unfailing light, then your kindness was thrown into relief, your love shone out more brightly, your grace was wider in its sweep. Star out of Jacob, how beautiful your rising above me![10]

And again:

> Even clad in my form, how beautiful you are, Lord Jesus! . . . Happy the man who, by attentive study of your life as a man among men, strives according to his strength to live like you. The Church in her loveliness has already received from you this blessed gift, the first fruits of her dowry; she is not slow to pattern herself on what is beautiful in you, nor ashamed to endure your ignominies.[11]

10. *SC*, CF 7:239.
11. *SC*, CF 7:57.

4

Jesus, the Truth of Our Lives

"I am . . . the truth." (John 14:6)

When we turn toward Jesus, however hesitatingly, and ponder all that he did for love of us, we begin to break through to a great truth: how much we mean to God, how much dignity we have in our creation as human beings, and what an immense capacity our soul has for the divine:

> The Word is righteousness from righteousness, wisdom from wisdom, truth from truth, as he is light from light and God from God. The soul is none of these, since it is not the image. Yet it is capable of them and yearns for them; that perhaps is why it is said to be made in the image. It is a lofty creature. In its capacity for greatness and in its longing we see a token of its uprightness.[1]

To the receptive heart Jesus presents himself as a teacher at this stage, saying, "Take my yoke upon you, and learn from me; for I am gentle and humble in heart" (Matt 11:29); the Image speaks to the image: "Become like me and you will truly become yourself." The taste of this truth, the truth of our capacity for God, is the great treasure discovered at the beginning of the journey. Up

1. *SC*, CF 40:146.

to this point our innate power of reason has been dulled, even blinded and asleep, and Jesus, a teacher passionate for truth, works particularly on this faculty in order to free it to become the power it was created to be in our interior. In the same light of truth by which we discover our beauty, we also begin to see the ways we have covered it up or distorted it or fallen from it. Honest self-reflection is demanded of us:

> The Son of God, the Word and Wisdom of the Father, mercifully assumed to himself human reason, the first of our powers. He found it oppressed by the flesh, held captive by sin, blinded by ignorance, distracted by outward things. He raised it by his might, taught it by his wisdom, drew it to things interior. More wonderfully still, he delegated to it his own power of Judge. To judge is the proper act of Truth and in this it [human reason] shared when out of reverence for the Word to which it is joined it became accuser, witness and judge against itself. Humility had been born from the union of the Word with human reason.[2]

It would be difficult to exaggerate the emphasis Saint Bernard puts on reflection leading to self-knowledge. In the *Steps of Humility and Pride* alone he speaks of self-scrutiny by personal experience of one's interior, sufficient attention to one's interior, recognition of one's evil and pitiable state, discernment of the truth within, sitting in judgment upon oneself, learning and perceiving one's incapacity.[3] He also gives realistic lists of the shadowy activity one finds within oneself: we are forever "bending to every breeze, trusting every spirit, bowing to flattery, flinching under fear, being upset by sadness, being shriveled by avarice, entangled by ambition, disquieted by suspicions, tormented by insults, exhausted by anxieties, puffed up by honors, consumed by envy";[4] and when he speaks of temptations and vices, the

2. *Hum*, CF 13A:48–49.
3. See *Hum*, CF 13A:41, 43, 45–46, 49.
4. See *SC*, CF 4:135.

many subtle distinctions he makes are clear evidence that he himself struggled long and hard with his eyes open.

According to Dom Bernardo Bonowitz, it is because of this insistence on attentiveness to one's interior, as opposed to curiosity, that Saint Bernard

> stands within the classical monastic tradition of *nepsis* and the Evagrian tradition that asserts that original sin was a consequence of negligence as much as of disobedience—or of a negligence that was disobedience in the light of the first commandment. To be a spiritual creature is to receive a responsibility to persevere in one's spiritual identity by a constant awareness of it and a constant fidelity to it. When we look inside ourselves without retaining the inward recollection of who we are, we run the risk of acting contrary to our nature or of letting the evil one slip into that central place of our heart and there exert an influence. This, by the way, is the basis for all monastic teaching about custody of the senses which, rather than being a dubious ascetical-penitential practice, is an essential contemplative activity—a 24-hour-a-day contemplative activity.[5]

This inward contemplative gaze in the light of truth, this careful guard of the heart and unflinching honesty about what we see there, clears a space within where it becomes increasingly easy to see, to hear, and to breathe the things of God. I recall that, about six months into my monastic postulancy, I reflected that even in that short time the guard of my heart had borne a fruit I would often describe in the words of the antiphon "Now the mind is filled with grace." Divine truth was beginning to invade me, freeing my reason and giving it joy, a joy flowing from the gifts that are proper to truth: clarity, certainty, humility, meaning, direction. If we persevere in this vigilant attentiveness, our hearts will eventually open to depths in which we experience being led by Jesus' own Spirit of Truth, who wishes us to do not even the slightest

5. Bernardo Bonowitz, OCSO, *Twelve Conferences on the Twelve Steps of Humility and the Twelve Steps of Pride,* given to the United States Cistercian Juniors, April, 2007, at Our Lady of the Holy Spirit Abbey, Conyers, Georgia.

thing without him. But, before we reach such depths, a fierce battle between enlightened reason and stubborn will must take place, a struggle described by Bernard with both practical wisdom and great humor:

> How reason and will engage in a dispute on behalf of the body. . . . Little old will gnashes her teeth. Her mind is maddened; she grows voluble, contentious and loud. She stalks out with her chest uncovered, her hair a tangle, and covered with horrible running sores. In such a state she accosts reason and shouts at him with great indignation: "Is this the kind of faith you keep with me? The servant is mine. I do not turn him over to you! He is mine. I still have him and will keep him a long time!" Reason soothes this angry viper, concealing what is going to happen until she has quieted down. Then reason introduces into the discussion matters other than those raised by will. "I have seen," he says, "a pleasure-garden with beautiful trees, and the sweetness of the place is beyond all delight. Would that you could rouse yourself and go there!"[6]

Truly the battle is as rough as this description—and even rougher. In another work Bernard describes the response of reason to rebellious will more realistically when he says that reason goes pale and is struck dumb with confusion, realizing how difficult the undertaking will be.[7] The trials for beginners are not so subtle as are those which beset proficients.[8] To flee adversity will be the overwhelming temptation at this point—and many do, in fact, flee. Yet steadfastness alone makes it possible for God's purifying truth to transform not only our minds but our entire selves; we must not only know the truth, we must also learn to walk in it—"learn how to live," as Saint Bernard would say.[9]

6. *The Parables and the Sentences*, CF 55 (Kalamazoo, MI: Cistercian Publications, 2000), 199–200.

7. See *Conv*, CF 25:42.

8. See *SC*, CF 31 (Kalamazoo, MI: Cistercian Publications, 1979), 169–70.

9. See *Sermo in festo ss. Apostolorum Petri et Pauli*, in *Sermons for the Summer Season*, CF 53:101.

In the process Jesus is teaching us another lesson, one that may be lost on us until after it bears fruit. The struggle with weakness and misery and the willingness to accept responsibility for what goes on in our interior begins to form in us a sympathetic heart, one that identifies with the weaknesses of others rather than blaming them. Bernard calls this a "second degree of truth": "This then is the second degree of truth, the one in which men look for it in their neighbors—when from the realization of their own shortcomings they discover those of other people and learn from their own painful experience to sympathize with those who suffer."[10]

In order not to lose our focus on the stages of prayer in Saint Bernard, we will not go into his very rich teaching on fraternal charity but will consider what in it touches on prayer or the experience of God. What seems clear is that Bernard came to the experience of God in others from below, not above; from within, not without. His was not a Damascus experience, that is, one in which the person of Jesus suddenly shines forth in identification with the other. The voice he hears is not primarily that of Jesus calling to him through human persons, the voice that so stirred Paul: "I am Jesus whom you are persecuting" (Acts 9:5). This voice is not absent in Bernard, for he alludes to Matthew 25:35-40 several times ("What you did to one of the least of these, you did to me"); but it is not his main emphasis when he speaks of love of neighbor. His starting point is more basic, as basic as the self, and it begins with the key text, "You shall love your neighbor as yourself" (Lev 19:18; Mt 19:19):

> If any man, conscious of his own sins, refuses to be angry when he sees a fellowman committing an offence, but instead approaches him with a love and sympathy that comfort him like the sweetest balsam, here is something whose source we know, but perhaps without grasping its significance. What I said is, when a man reflects on his own conduct he ought to feel impelled to be gentle with all. Following the wise counsel of Saint Paul, he must learn to love those who are caught in

10. *Hum,* CF 13A:46.

> habits of sin, not forgetting that he himself is open to temptation. Is it not in this very thing that love of neighbor is rooted, as the commandment reveals: "You must love your neighbor as yourself"?[11]

From within our own hearts, where we have known the mercy of Jesus toward us, we look out toward others, our "eyes resting with loving-kindness" upon them in their manifold miseries and weaknesses.[12] It is as if Christ's kind, clear eyes become our eyes for beholding both ourselves and others, and in this way he becomes increasingly the very truth of our lives.

> *"Enter not into judgment with your servant."*
> *May he enter as one who brings peace, joy and gladness;*
> *but may he also enter with the gravity of maturity*
> *to purify my joy and control my arrogance*
> *with the stern gaze of truth.*
> *May he come as a leaping fawn and a sharp-eyed roe,*
> *to pass over my offences and look at them*
> *only with pity and forgiveness.*[13]

11. *SC*, CF 7:227.
12. *SC*, CF 4:77.
13. *SC*, CF 40:96.

5

At the Feet of Jesus

She stood behind him at his feet, weeping, and began to bathe his feet with her tears and to dry them with her hair. Then she continued kissing his feet and anointing them with the ointment. (Luke 7:38)

Bernard's imagery for the first of the "three stages of the soul's progress"[1] is appropriately expressive of something foundational: that low and lovely place defined by a sinful woman's many kisses and her anointing of the Lord's feet. This first stage is that of the broken, contrite heart receiving the forgiveness of sins, while Bernard's favored image for it is the penitent woman lying in the dust at Jesus' feet,[2] a person who models for us the dispositions described so far. Pierced by the pain of her sinful life, drawn by the beauty and humble approachability of Jesus, she has turned her passionate love in the right direction, faced the truth of her interior life, and bowed down before him in love and sorrow, surrendering her whole life—past, present, future—to his mercy.

Throughout our lives we return to this place, failing, prostrating before the Lord in sorrow, then rising, uplifted by his hand. But there is a time in our prayer life when we are predominantly here at his feet, even if we have not been Mary Magdalenes. When he

1. *SC*, CF 4:21
2. See *SC*, CF 4:17, 34–35, 53–54, 82.

who enlightens everyone who comes into the world begins to fill our souls with the knowledge of who he is and who we are and are not, the natural response of both body and soul is to prostrate themselves before him in sorrow, awaiting his word of forgiveness which alone can set us free and make us new:

> She wept bitterly, she sighed deeply from her heart, she sobbed with a repentance that shook her very being, till the evil that inflamed her passions was cleansed away. The heavenly physician came with speed to her aid, because "his word runs swiftly." Perhaps you think the Word of God is not a medicine? Surely it is, a medicine strong and pungent, testing the mind and the heart. . . . It is up to you, wretched sinner, to humble yourself as this happy penitent did so that you may be rid of your wretchedness. Prostrate yourself on the ground, take hold of his feet, soothe them with kisses, sprinkle them with your tears and so wash not them but yourself. Thus you will become one of the "flock of shorn ewes as they come up from the washing." But even then you may not dare to lift up a face suffused with shame and grief, until you hear the sentence: "Your sins are forgiven."[3]

> See how, prostrate at his human feet, the penitent finds assurance as she is told: "Your sins are forgiven." . . . God removes the sin of the one who makes humble confession, and thereby the devil loses the sovereignty he had gained over the human heart.[4]

Our experience may not be as immediate and cathartic as hers, but this stage will always be one of humbling truth leading to greater groundedness in reality and less self-centeredness. Like me, you may find yourself suddenly cringing with embarrassment at the fleeting memory of something you said or did when you thought you were the center of the universe—a thought that reveals itself as much in self-rejection as in self-exaltation. In addition, this humbling truth grows within the context of community

3. *SC*, CF 4:17.
4. *SC*, CF 4:34.

(recall Bernard's description of his beginnings in the monastery), for God loves interdependence. We see our possibilities, we see our blocks, and we hear about our blind spots through those personal "mirrors" we encounter every day, be they our family members, community members, friends, colleagues, and so forth. And, at the heart of each of our particular communities, God provides one or two to accompany us more intimately and fully, someone who can speak the truth to us in love or, rather, someone through whom God has chosen to speak to us that truth. As Bernard says, "Each and every person must have his Moses, under whose guidance and direction he may depart from Egypt."[5]

The question will naturally arise concerning the length of this stage. How do we know when we are passing to another? Granted that so much depends here on personal grace and unique call, there are at least two helpful principles I have discovered in Bernard:

1. Trust the movement in the heart which urges one to draw closer to God.
2. Avoid the spiritual and psychological imbalance of concentrating excessively on one's sinfulness.

In regard to the first, trusting the desire to be closer to the Lord, Bernard couldn't possibly be stronger in his conviction that this is the Lord's desire as well. Many texts attest to this; for instance: "Yesterday you were lifted from the mud, today you wish to encounter the glory of his face? No, his hand must be your guide to that end. First it must cleanse your stains, then it must raise you up. How raise you? By giving you the grace to dare to aspire."[6] And the following seems to be the boldest text of all in this area:

> We have seen how every soul—even if burdened with sin, enmeshed in vice, ensnared by the allurements of pleasure, a captive in exile, imprisoned in the body, caught in the mud, fixed

5. *Sent*, CF 55:199–200.
6. *SC*, CF 4:19.

> in mire, bound to its members, a slave to care, distracted by business, afflicted with sorrow, wandering and straying, filled with anxious forebodings and uneasy suspicions, a stranger in a hostile land, and, according to the Prophet, sharing the defilement of the dead and counted with those who go down into hell—every soul, I say, standing thus under condemnation and without hope, has the power to turn and find it can not only breathe the fresh air of pardon and mercy, but also dare to aspire to the nuptials of the Word, not fearing to enter into alliance with God or to bear the sweet yoke of love with the King of angels.[7]

If we stay close to our hearts, dwelling in quietness and trust, we will be sure to hear the voice that tells us to "dare to aspire" to deeper intimacy. It cannot be anticipated, but when it comes, it cannot be disregarded without real personal loss.

In regard to the second principle, here we meet the incredible balance and delicate discretion of Saint Bernard. A healthy tension is meant to exist in our lives between sorrow for sin and thanksgiving, between justice and mercy, what Bernard calls the two feet of the Lord.[8]

> And for that reason my advice to you, my friends, is to turn aside occasionally from troubled and anxious pondering on the paths you may be treading, and to travel on smoother ways where the gifts of God may be serenely savored, so that the thought of him may give breathing space to you whose consciences are perplexed. . . . Sorrow for sin is indeed necessary, but it should not be an endless preoccupation. You must dwell also on the glad remembrance of God's loving-kindness.[9]

> And if, as happened at times, I should grow forgetful of his mercy, and with a stricken conscience become too deeply involved in the thought of judgment, sooner or later I was cast down in unbelievable fear and shameful misery: "Who has felt

7. *SC*, CF 40:180–81.
8. See *SC*, CF 4:36–37.
9. *SC*, CF 4:70.

> the full force of your fury, or learnt to fear the violence of your rage?" But if on escaping from this I should cling more than was becoming to the foot of mercy, the opposite happened. I became dissipated, indifferent, negligent; lukewarm at prayer, languid at work, always on the watch for a laugh, inclined to say the wrong thing. And my interior was no steadier than my behavior. But you know what a teacher experience is; no longer of judgment alone or mercy alone, but of mercy and judgment I will sing to you, O Lord.[10]

This then is a sign that one is ready to rise and run after the Lord, when one knows deep sorrow for sin, but knows as well mercy and thanksgiving. "He cannot but bear upon him the imprint of the divine footsteps,"[11] both footsteps. Jesus rises in us, he walks, he runs; and in order to follow him we must do likewise.

Of this penitent woman who lay prostrate in the dust, image of our soul, we read in John's Gospel: "Mary Magdalene . . . saw that the stone had been removed from the tomb. So she ran and went to Simon Peter and the other disciple, the one whom Jesus loved" (John 20:1-2). And in Matthew's Gospel: "So they [Mary Magdalene and the other Mary] left the tomb quickly with fear and great joy, and ran to tell his disciples" (Matt 28:8). The stage of the tomb must be embraced, but when the divine footsteps press upon our hearts we must run with all the joy of someone in love, praying with Bernard:

> So let us run and run,
> but in the odor of your ointments,
> not by trusting in our own worth.
> We pin our hopes for the race
> not in the durability of our own powers
> but in the abundance of your mercies.[12]

10. *SC*, CF 4:37.
11. *SC*, CF 4:36.
12. *SC*, CF 7:12.

Stage Two

With the advancement of the day you gave your servant reason to rejoice when, in the kiss of your hand, you imparted the grace to live rightly.[1]

1. *SC*, CF 4:20.

6

Love's Claim

Stage Two of our journey of prayer begins and actually continues where Stage One ended, namely, in the experience of Jesus in the flesh—his human beauty, humility, and vulnerability. The differences between the two stages lie in the quality of our responses to Jesus, now that our hearts have undergone some degree of purification. Nothing could illustrate this better than a threefold consideration that seems to have been a real preoccupation with Bernard:

1. God created us with great ease.
2. He recreated us with extreme personal difficulty.
3. This labor of re-creation is meant to involve us in a debt that only great love and gratitude can pay.

To capture the power and persistence of this spiritual syllogism, so central to Bernard, I will offer certain illustrative texts side by side at the end of the chapter. In this way the unique beauty of each one will be seen alongside their strong common thrust. But I now cite the longest and, to my mind, the most beautiful of such texts:

> Now with regard to the manner, which if you remember, we defined as God's self-emptying, I venture to offer three important points for your consideration. For that emptying was neither a simple gesture nor a limited one; but he emptied himself

even to the assuming of human nature, even to accepting death, death on a cross. Who is there who can adequately gauge the greatness of the humility, gentleness, self-surrender, revealed by the Lord of majesty in assuming human nature, in accepting the punishment of death, the shame of the cross? But somebody will say: "Surely the Creator could have restored his original plan without all that hardship?" Yes, he could, but he chose the way of personal suffering so that man would never again have a reason to display that worst and most hateful of vices, ingratitude. If his decision did involve painful weariness for himself, it was meant also to involve man in a debt that only great love can pay. Where the ease with which man was created sapped his spirit of devotion, the hardship with which he was redeemed should urge him on to gratitude. For how did man the ingrate regard his creation? I was created freely indeed with no trouble or labor on my Creator's part; for at his command I was made, just like every other thing. What is big about that gift if not the facility of the word that made it?" Thus does human impiety belittle the boon of creation, and turn that which of its nature is a source of love into an occasion for ingratitude. Those who live by these sentiments share the godlessness of evil-doers. But these lying mouths are silenced. For, *more obvious than the light of day is the immense sacrifice he has made for you, O Man; he who was Lord became a slave, he who was rich became a pauper, the Word was made flesh, and the Son of God did not disdain to become the son of man. So may it please you to remember that, even if made out of nothing, you have not been redeemed out of nothing*. In six days he created all things, and among them, you. On the other hand, for a period of thirty years he worked out your salvation in the midst of the earth. What endurance was his in those labors! To his bodily needs and the molestations of his enemies did he not add the mightier burden of the ignominy of the cross, and crown it all with the horror of his death? And this was indeed necessary. Man and beast you save, O Lord. How you have multiplied your mercy, O God![1]

1. *SC*, CF 4:74–75 (emphasis added).

The message is powerfully and passionately clear. If we are ever to become truly ourselves, that is, to be restored to the ability to love God with a pure, uncalculating, grateful, humble, uncomplaining, absolute, deeply affectionate, and intensely joyful love, then we have to see such a love with our own eyes. It was necessary that Jesus restore us in the precise way he did because, although theoretically God could have saved us in a way less painful to himself, concretely he was dealing with the resistant human heart, a heart that needed to taste and see and be burned to its depths by Jesus' way of living. When this truth stirs us interiorly, we hear a call that honors us beyond all imagining. We hear him say, "Risk everything, lose everything and love as I have loved you, for I have involved you 'in a debt that only great love can pay.'" What emerges at this moment in our prayer is devotion, the beginning of heartfelt devotion to the person of Jesus for his own sake—our first steps, so to speak, toward the fullness of loving response to his merciful love for us. It is the divine mercy that evokes in our own hearts the desire to return love for love.

Bernard spent himself completely on enkindling and sustaining this devotion in his monks by preaching Christ crucified: "As you well know, these sentiments are often on my lips, and God knows they are always in my heart. They are a familiar theme in my writings, as is evident. This is my philosophy, one more refined and interior, to know Jesus and him crucified."[2] It is clear that he had experienced Jesus at another depth, a depth to which he longed to return; yet his care for his brothers and his desire that Jesus be known and loved gave him the energy to put aside his own interests for theirs as he led them to the wounds that would provide the only solid foundation for their spiritual growth.[3] The following passage from *Sermon 61* expresses this so eloquently that even those who are not attracted by Saint Bernard or his style admit to its sheer power and beauty:

2. *SC*, CF 7:223.
3. See *SC*, CF 7:15–16.

> Where is there safe, sure rest for the weak except in the Saviour's wounds? There the security of my dwelling depends on the greatness of his saving power. The world rages, the body oppresses, the devil lays his snares: I do not fall because I am founded on a rock. I have sinned gravely, my conscience is disturbed but not confounded, because I shall remember the wounds of the Lord. For "he was wounded for our transgressions." . . . Whatever is lacking in my own resources I appropriate for myself from the heart of the Lord, which overflows with mercy. And there is no lack of clefts by which they are poured out. They pierced his hands and his feet, they gored his side with a lance, and through these fissures I can suck honey from the rock and oil from the flinty stone—I can taste and see that the Lord is good. He was thinking thoughts of peace and I did not know it. "For who has known the mind of the Lord, or who has been his counselor?" But the nail that pierced him has become for me a key unlocking the sight of the Lord's will. Why should I not gaze through the cleft? The nail cries out, the wound cries out that God is truly in Christ reconciling the world to himself. "The iron pierced his soul" and his heart has drawn near, so that he is no longer one who cannot sympathize with my weaknesses. The secret of his heart is laid open through the clefts of his body; that mighty mystery of loving is laid open, laid open to the tender mercies of our God, in which the morning sun from on high has risen upon us. Surely his heart is laid open through his wounds![4]

And so we embark on the path by which we begin to return love for love.

According to Bernard there are definite stages in this return, and, therefore, I have chosen as a point of reference what he calls the "process of infusion" with its seven rather inclusive steps:

> I wish to remind you now of the principles necessary for our salvation and how to apply them, the truths that must be infused into us and their order of importance. . . . We need first of all compunction of heart [*compunctio*], then, fervor of spirit [*devotio*];

4. *SC*, CF 31:142–44.

> thirdly, the labor of penance [*pœnitentiæ labor*]; fourthly, works of charity [*pietatis opus*]; fifthly, zeal for prayer [*orationis studium*]; sixthly, leisure for contemplation [*contemplationis otium*]; seventhly, love in all its fullness [*plenitudo dilectionis*]. All these are the work of one and the same Spirit, accomplished by the process called infusion.[5]

If "compunction," the first infusion, belongs properly to the first stage of prayer and "contemplation" and the "fullness of love" to the third stage, those in between are the substance of this middle stage, which the person devoted to Jesus now enters.

Additional Texts on This Theme

I

> If I owe everything for having been created, what can I add for being remade, and being remade in this way? It was less easy to remake me than to make me. It is written not only about me but of every created being: "He spoke and they were made." But he who made me by a single word, in remaking me had to speak many words, work miracles, suffer hardships, and not only hardships but even unjust treatment. "What shall I render to the Lord for all that he has given me?" In his first work he gave me myself; in his second work he gave me himself; when he gave me himself, he gave me back myself. Given, and regiven, I owe myself twice over. What can I give God in return for himself? Even if I could give him myself a thousand times, what am I to God?[6]

II

> But there is something else that moves me, arouses and enflames me even more. Good Jesus, the chalice you drank, the price of our redemption, makes me love you more than all the rest. This alone would be enough to claim our love. This, I say, is what wins our love so sweetly, justly demands it, firmly binds it,

5. *SC*, CF 4:137–39.
6. *Dil*, CF 13B:18.

deeply affects it. Our Savior had to toil so hard in this, in fact in making the whole world the Creator did not labor so much. Then "he spoke and they were made; he commanded and they were created." But in saving us he had to endure men who contradicted his words, criticized his actions, ridiculed his sufferings, and mocked his death. See how much he loved us.[7]

III

The Apostle says explicitly that "Christ dwells by faith in our hearts." No need to be surprised that the Lord Jesus should be pleased to dwell in this heaven, which he not only called into being by his word like the other creatures, but fought to acquire and died to redeem. And when his passion was over the longing of his heart found echo in the words: "This is my resting-place for ever; here will I dwell, for I have desired it."[8]

IV

See, therefore, O man, what great things the Majesty of God has done for you. With regard to all the things that are in heaven or under heaven, he merely "spoke and they were made, he commanded and they were created." What is easier than to speak a word? But although he created you with a mere word, was it with a mere word you were recreated? For three and thirty years "he was seen upon earth and conversed with men," who only took occasion from his actions and words to slander and insult him; and to such straits was he reduced that he "had no where to lay his head." . . . My brethren, the Lord Jesus has embraced us by taking upon himself our labors and sorrows; let us in return embrace him with the two arms, so to speak, of patience and purity of intention, by acting and suffering for justice's sake, by directing our actions according to the rule of justice, and by bearing our sorrows for the love of justice. Let us also say with the Spouse in the Canticle, "I held him and I

7. *SC*, CF 4:148.
8. *SC*, CF 7:82.

will not let him go." And let us say with the Patriarch, "I will not let you go except you bless me."[9]

V

Truly indeed these two graces (creation and being continually sustained by the Creator) are doubly gratuitous. Why do I say "doubly gratuitous"? Without deserving on your part, or effort on his. "For he spoke and it was done." Are we to be less devout, less indebted, less thankful because he made them out of nothing and for nothing? I do not think either of these gifts is any less useful just because it was less difficult to bestow. . . . And now mark the third work: your redemption. There is no excuse for ingratitude; great effort went into it. Freely was it accomplished, but free on your part. Clearly it was not without cost to him. You were saved for nothing, but not by nothing. How can affection doze in these circumstances? What is more, it has died out; it is not merely dozing when it fails to respond to so great a benefit, when it does not pour itself out in thanksgiving and songs of praise. This third gift very clearly gauges the other two and proves that true love underlay them, and it is easily eminent not because he did not choose to do it in some other way, but because no other way was suitable. So then, your God made you, and he made many things for your benefit, and he even, as it were, made himself for you: "The Word was made flesh and dwelt among us." What was left after that?[10]

9. *Sermo in feria iv hebdomadæ sanctæ*, in *Saint Bernard's Sermons for the Seasons and Principal Festivals of the Year,* vol. 2, trans. A. Luddy (Dublin: Browne and Nolan Ltd., 1923), 150–51, 153.

10. *QH*, CF 25:231–32.

7

Devotion: What Return Can I Make to the Lord?

Saint Bernard and our Cistercian fathers understand devotion as the wholehearted and heartfelt gift of self to God.[1] A number of years ago I participated in an interreligious dialogue on the theme of emptiness. Afterward, in response to some comments I made, someone stated that it had been a long time since he had thought of religion in terms of devotion. I replied that our Cistercian way actually had few "devotions," but he replied in turn: "No, I mean devotion to a person, to the person of Jesus, so evident in your talk." This is surely the heart of devotion as understood by Bernard: personal, deeply felt, relational.

Devotio follows *compunctio,* not only here in the steps of infusion, but elsewhere in Bernard's thinking. When Bernard considers the soul's progress under the image of the three ointments, devotion stands between compunction and loving-kindness (*pietas*):

> [Devotion] is that religious attitude in which the benefits of God are recalled with gladness and thanksgiving. . . . It was with special reference to this anointing that the Prophet exclaimed: "How good, how delightful it is for all to live together like brothers; fine as oil on the head." These words do not seem

1. See Edith Scholl, "'Kindness and Faithfulness Shall Meet': *Devotio* and *Pietas,*" *Cistercian Studies Quarterly,* 32, no. 3 (1997): 304–5.

> applicable to the first anointing. Though that is good in itself, it is not by any means pleasant, because the recollection of one's sins begets bitterness rather than pleasure. Nor do those involved in it live together, since each one bewails and mourns over his particular sins. Those, however, who are employed in the work of thanksgiving are contemplating and thinking about God alone, and so they cannot help but dwell in unity.[2]

Note how devotion is here linked to the prayer of thanksgiving. We find the same connection in *Sermon 18,* in which the person filled with devotion pours out words of thanks: "You have loosed my bond. I will offer you the thanksgiving sacrifice."[3] And in another sermon we read, "The speech of the Word is loving-kindness, that of the soul, the fervor of devotion. . . . The speech of the Word is an infusion of grace, the soul's response is wonder and thanksgiving."[4] The importance of this prayer of thanksgiving cannot be overestimated in Saint Bernard's thought.

Let us consider more in depth Bernard's words on gratitude in the passages quoted above, in connection with the great labor the Lord endured in recreating us:

> Surely the Creator could have restored his original plan without all that hardship? Yes, he could, but he chose the way of personal suffering so that man would never again have a reason to display that worst and most hateful of vices, ingratitude. . . . Where the ease with which man was created sapped his spirit of devotion, the hardship with which he was redeemed should urge him on to gratitude. . . . For how did man the ingrate regard his creation? "I was created freely indeed with no trouble or labor on my Creator's part; for at his command I was made, just like every other thing. What is big about that gift if not the facility of the word that made it?" Thus does human impiety belittle the boon of creation, and turn that which of its nature

2. *SC,* CF 4:69.
3. *SC,* CF 4:137.
4. *SC,* CF 7:238.

> is a source of love into an occasion for ingratitude. Those who live by these sentiments share the godlessness of evil-doers.[5]

> "What shall I render to the Lord for all that he has given to me?" In his first work he gave me myself; in his second work he gave me himself; when he gave me himself, he gave me back myself. Given and regiven, I owe myself twice over. What can I give God in return for himself?[6]

> Are we to be less devout, less indebted, less thankful because he made them out of nothing and for nothing? I do not think either of these gifts is any less useful just because it was less difficult to bestow. . . . And now mark the third work: your redemption. There is no excuse for ingratitude. . . . How can affection doze in these circumstances? What is more, it has died out; it is not merely dozing when it fails to respond to so great a benefit, when it does not pour itself out in thanksgiving and songs of praise.[7]

These thoughts, so true and so strong, should shock us into reality. Fr. Charles Dumont has captured in some wonderful pages the significance of the prayer of thanksgiving in Saint Bernard, stating that thanksgiving for the work of grace, especially the painful labor involved in our redemption, opens up to "intimate conversation, which consists essentially in astonished reflection on God's action [in our lives]. . . . So Bernard can say that the Word's language is the gift of grace (*infusio doni*) and the soul's response is its surprise, which is expressed in thanksgiving."[8] Hopefully, we can all look back on at least one time in our lives when, like David, we went before the Lord and asked in utter amazement: "Who am I, Lord God, that you have done this for me?" (1 Sam 7:18).

Yet so much depends on reflection, on remembering or forgetting, on sensitivity to the gift or presumption, on taking as much

5. *SC*, CF 4:74–75.
6. *Dil*, CF 13B:108.
7. *QH*, CF 25:231.
8. Charles Dumont, *Pathway of Peace*, CS 187 (Kalamazoo, MI: Cistercian Publications, 1999), 223.

time to thank God for answering our prayers as we did to petition him, on savoring the gift rather than anxiously flying off to our next request. In order that thanksgiving become a state of grace, as Fr. Charles calls it, one must make continual efforts to actually live in thanksgiving, since ingratitude, "that worst and most hateful of vices," crouches at our door. He quotes another passage from Bernard that strongly confirms this thought:

> Even today we see many people who insistently ask for what they realize they need, but we know very few who give thanks in proportion to what they have received. There is nothing reprehensible about insistent petition, but if we show that we are ungrateful we nullify the effects of what we asked for. . . . We are sorry to say that we see many [monks] who think that, as long as they continue to wear the habit and are tonsured, they are completely safe. They are not aware of how the worm of ingratitude is gnawing at them inside. . . . Haven't they been gradually falling away? . . . A number of them are secretly afflicted with an ulcer worse than this leprosy [of worldly life]: ingratitude, which is all the more dangerous because it is hidden. . . . When we show that we are not ungrateful for the gifts we have received, we prepare a place in ourselves for grace, so that we may receive still greater gifts. It is ingratitude, and ingratitude alone, which prevents us from progressing in our Christian commitment. . . . When we are at the beginning [of our conversion] we feel like strangers (like the leper and the Samaritan woman) and disclose that we are full of fear, fervor and humility. But later on we easily forget the gratuitous nature of everything we have received and become abusively presumptuous about our familiarity with God. . . . What God requires of us is not words, but an *act* of thanksgiving.[9]

I have reflected often that if the first stage is characterized in its fullness by an abiding sorrow for sin, the second is characterized by an abiding gratitude for the treasure hidden in every moment, even, and perhaps especially, the painful moments. The

9. Dumont, *Pathway of Peace*, CS 187:226–27.

one who always seeks always finds this treasure. But to be grateful always, abidingly thankful, is not easily attained. What sorrows and losses we have to bear in life, our own and those of the persons dearest to us! To do so with patience is often the most virtue we can manage. In addition, what struggles we have to endure with our complaining, distrustful, self-centered dispositions before we are thankful always! As Bernard says:

> As to the fourth form of prayer, thanksgiving, I believe that few reach it. It is all the more precious in being more infrequent. It is an abundant grace which a human being who has arrived at this point finds in God directly, in virtue of God's promise to answer even before being invoked. The Spirit received from God attests to this person's spirit that its desire has been heard."[10]

Even though few reach it, it is important to be journeying toward it steadily. Dom Paschal of Spencer, who was our chaplain at Mt. Saint Mary's for seven years, shared with us an invaluable tool: to thank God for a favor received as often as you petitioned for it, or, as Bernard put it, to give thanks in proportion as you have received. Try it. The result is a sense of perspective in which the weightier things in life fall into their rightful place, dead center, and the less weighty order themselves around that center. In choosing to be conscious of the enormous gifts we have received, we can bear our difficulties with a deeper sense that God, who has come through for us again and again, will be with us no matter what.

As one grows in this prayer of grateful love, a question wells up again and again in the depths of our hearts as it did in Bernard's, a question that is actually more an exclamation of surprise and wonder: "What shall I return to the Lord for all his bounty to me?" (Ps 116:12). The psalm itself gives the answer—gratitude, immense gratitude: "I will offer you a thanksgiving sacrifice" (Ps 116:17).

10. Dumont, *Pathway of Peace*, CS 187:223.

How wonderful your love for me,
my God, my love!
How wonderful your love for me,
everywhere mindful of me,
everywhere eager for the welfare of one who is needy and poor.
I will sing, I will sing to the Lord as long as I live.
I will sing praise to my God while I have being.
How great are his powers,
what wonders has he not done![11]

11. *SC*, CF 4:131.

8

Keeping Vigil

After the infusion of devotion, so filled with thanksgiving, Saint Bernard places the infusion of penance: "fastings, vigils, prayers, and other tasks that penitents perform." Let us focus particularly on "vigils," since his development of the vigilant heart is profound.

By "vigils" Bernard refers to the Cistercian practice of rising long before dawn to wait with the Lord and for the Lord, to watch in prayer that we may be ready to open the door of our heart as soon as he knocks: "He says, 'I love those who love me and they who seek me early shall find me.' . . . Do you keep watch? He keeps watch also. If you rise at night before the time of vigils and hasten to anticipate the morning, you will find him there. He will always be waiting for you."[1]

However ordinary, obscure, and laborious Cistercian life may be, the mystery of the night holds this abiding secret, difficult to speak of because it is so secret: God is faithful to his promise; those who seek him early find him in a way that leaves no room for doubt, at least not for long, in a way that makes us hunger and thirst for more:

> Anyone who chooses to pray must choose not only the right place but also the right time. A time of leisure is best and most convenient, the deep silence when others are asleep is particularly

1. *SC*, CF 40:35.

> suitable, for prayer will then be freer and purer. "Arise at the first watch of the night, and pour out your heart like water before the face of the Lord, your God." How secretly prayer goes up in the night, witnessed only by God and the holy angel who received it to present it at the heavenly altar! How pleasing, how unclouded it is, colored with the blush of modesty! How serene, how calm, free from noise and interruption! How pure it is, how sincere, unsullied by the dust of earthly care, untouched by ostentation or human flattery! . . . You will not pray aright, if in your prayers you seek anything but the Word, or seek him for the sake of anything but the Word; for in him are all things. In him is healing for your wounds, help in your need, restoration for your faults, resources for further growth; in him is all that men should ask or desire, all they need, all that will profit them. There is no reason to ask anything else of the Word, for he is all.[2]

Such a practice forms in us day by day, little by little, a disposition of continual watchfulness, abiding attentiveness. I described this in the first stage as a careful guard over all the movements of the heart, and I also mentioned there that as we persevere in interior vigilance, our hearts begin to open to even greater depths of awareness, for the Spirit searches everything, even the depths of God:

> Let us return now to ourselves, let us examine our paths; and in order to accomplish this in truth, let us invoke the Spirit of truth, let us call to him from the deep into which he has led us, because he leads us on the way by which we discover ourselves, and without him we can do nothing. Nor should we be afraid that he will disdain to come down to us, for the contrary is true: he is displeased if we attempt even the least thing without him.[3]

One of my first profound realizations of this truth, that is, of the depths of watchfulness to which we are called, involved my early experiences of solitary days in the community hermitage. I somehow thought that this day away from the common life would be a day to be free for whatever good thing I wanted to do with

2. *SC*, CF 40:213–14.
3. *SC*, CF 4:132.

my time. But my heart, formed by monastic life if only for a few years, knew better. As soon as I got in the door I realized that the Spirit had a plan for our day, an absolutely wonderful plan, and to follow it I would need to stay close to my heart and to pray often to follow his leading. That is the way it is really meant to be—that he have his way in us—"because he leads us on the way by which we discover ourselves."[4]

But, reminds Bernard, the Spirit comes and goes as he wills and has alternations of silence and speech, absence and presence, alternations by which he is forming us spiritually, stretching us beyond the limits of our human understanding. Fr. Michael Casey has an excellent treatment of the wisdom involved in these alternations in promoting true growth. Particularly relevant to the experience of prayer is the following:

> It is only after this mortal life that such an interplay of presence and absence will terminate. Meanwhile, desire is increased by the experience of absence and with each subsequent return the union between the soul and the Word becomes a little stronger and more intense. As the soul grows in the recognition of its own resourcelessness, its dependence on God increases and it becomes progressively detached from other sources of support. But it is only through the experience of bitter desolation that this comes about.[5]

In my own experience of these alternations of the Spirit, I have often asked myself what to do when he seems silent. The following is one of the most important principles of prayer I have learned from Saint Bernard, a principle I have paraphrased in a way that has helped me thousands of times:

> When the Spirit speaks, act.
> When the Spirit is silent, wait.

4. *SC*, CF 4:132.

5. Michael Casey, *Athirst for God: Spiritual Desire in Bernard of Clairvaux's Sermons on the Song of Songs*, CS 77 (Kalamazoo, MI: Cistercian Publications, 1988), 264.

Wait, for he will surely come, surely give the light you need. But in the meantime, learn neither to impose nor create your own answer. Learn to listen for that voice of certain truth:

> Either let the Holy Spirit always speak, a procedure that no influence of ours can procure; or let him at least warn us when he withdraws into silence, that his very silence may then be our guide; otherwise, mistakenly thinking he is still leading us on, we shall pursue with disastrous assurance an erroneous course of our own.[6]

The more we learn to trust this most reliable of guides, the more surely we proceed to our interior and the more securely our choices and actions flow from a deep heart. Jesus has given us his own Spirit to accompany us at every single moment of our long night's vigil on this earth:

> And lest you complain or sorrow at my absence, I will send you the Spirit, the Paraclete, who will give you the pledge of salvation, the force of life, and the light of knowledge. He will give you the pledge of salvation, that the Spirit himself may bear witness that you are a child of God. He will show you and impress upon your heart unmistakable signs of your predestination. He will put gladness in your heart, and with the dew of heaven will satisfy your mind, if not constantly, then very often. He will give the force of life that what is by nature impossible for you will, through his grace, be made not only possible but even easy. Then you will proceed with delight, as in all riches, in labors, in vigils, in hunger and thirst, and in all observances which, unless sweetened with this meal, may seem to be death in the pot. He will give you the light of knowledge so that when you have done all things well you may consider yourself an unprofitable servant; and whatever good you find in yourself you may attribute to him from whom comes all good and without whom you cannot begin, much less complete, even the smallest task.[7]

6. *SC*, CF 4:128.
7. *Sermo in die Pentecostes*, in *Sermons for the Summer Season*, CF 53:78.

9

The Prayers

The third infusion speaks also of prayers *(orationes)*. In fact, the entire phrase "fastings, vigils, prayers" recalls the First Conference of Cassian where the same threesome is mentioned. The context is significant:

> It is largely up to us whether the character of our thoughts improves and whether either holy and spiritual thoughts or earthly and carnal ones increase in our hearts. Therefore we practice the frequent reading of and constant meditation on Scripture, so that we may be open to a spiritual point of view. For this reason we frequently chant the psalms, so that we may continually grow in compunction. For this reason we are diligent in vigils, fasting and praying, so that the mind which has been stretched to its limits may not taste earthly things but contemplate heavenly ones.[1]

Cassian is recommending those practices by which we cooperate in the purification of our minds, and Bernard also speaks of these practices as a medicine.

What specifically are "the prayers"? For one thing, it is likely they include the psalms which are part of Cassian's context and which, after they have been chanted in common, are meant to be sung in the heart. Indeed, in his very first sermon on the Song of Songs, Bernard gives a beautiful description of how our soul can

1. John Cassian, *The Conferences*, translated and annotated by Boniface Ramsey, Ancient Christian Writers 57 (New York: Paulist Press, 1997), 56–57.

be shaped by the psalms if we take care to relate our own experiences to the psalmist's:

> If you look back at your own experience, is it not in that victory by which your faith overcomes the world, in "your exit from the horrible pit and out of the slough of the marsh," that you yourselves sing a new song to the Lord for all the marvels he has performed? Again, when he purposed to "settle your feet on a rock and to direct your steps," then too, I feel certain a new song was sounding on your lips, a song to our God for his gracious renewal of your life. When you repented he not only forgave your sins but even promised rewards so that, rejoicing in the hope of benefits to come, you sing of the Lord's ways: how great is the glory of the Lord! And when, as happens, texts of Scripture hitherto dark and impenetrable at last become bright with meaning for you, then in gratitude for this nurturing bread of heaven you must charm the ears of God with a voice of exultation and praise, a festal song. In the daily trials and combats arising from the flesh, the world and the devil, that are never wanting to those who live devout lives in Christ, you learn by experience that man's life on earth is a ceaseless warfare, and are impelled to repeat your songs day after day for every victory won. As often as temptation is overcome, an immoral habit brought under control, an impending danger shunned, the trap of the seducer detected, when a passion long indulged is finally and perfectly allayed, or a virtue persistently desired and repeatedly sought is ultimately obtained by God's gift; so often, in the words of the prophet, let thanksgiving and joy resound. For every benefit conferred, God is to be praised in his gifts. Otherwise when the time of judgment comes, that man will be punished as an ingrate who cannot say to God: "Your statutes were my song in the land of exile."[2]

Here Bernard stands in the tradition of ancient monastic wisdom, which called monks to be awakened by the psalms, to live inside them, and to meet Jesus there. It was a modern Cistercian who first touched my own heart with the desire to explore this path so full of presence and hope:

2. *SC*, CF 4:5–6.

> Many of the Psalms are most appropriate for times of suffering and trial. . . . At such times, our souls need strength and can seek it in such Psalms as Psalm 12: "How long, O Lord, wilt thou utterly forget me? How long wilt thou hide Thy face from me?" Or Psalm 30: "For I have heard the hissing of the crowd—terror is everywhere! Assembling together against me, they planned to take away my life." Here again, in our sufferings and perils, we find ourselves united with the Mysterious Companion who looms up at our side, or indeed within the depths of our soul, as we recite the Psalms. It is Christ who has suffered before us, and for us. He has come to us in the Psalm. If we had not recited it, perhaps we would not have found Him at all, and we might have gone our way into despair.[3]

Prayed within the Divine Office itself, the psalms are part of a liturgy where heaven and earth meet in joyous and intimate communion and where the possibilities for the experience of interior prayer are great:

> One who seeks access to the interior of the home goes round to the intimate friends or members of the household to attain what he desires. In this present instance who might these people be? In my opinion they are the holy angels who wait on us as we pray, who offer to God the petitions and desires of men, at least of those men whose prayer they recognize to be sincere, free from anger and dissension. That the holy angels do condescend to mingle with us when we praise God in psalmody is very clearly stated by the Psalmist: "The princes went before, joined with the singer, in the midst of young damsels playing on timbrels." He also said: "I will sing praise to you in the sight of the angels." . . . Be mindful then of these angelic princes when you go to pray or to sing the psalms; stand with disciplined reverence and be proud that your angels continuously see the face of the Father. Since they are all spirits whose work is service sent to help those who will be the heirs of salvation, they bear our prayers to God in heaven and return laden with graces for us. Let us make use

3. Thomas Merton, *Praying the Psalms* (Collegeville, MN: Liturgical Press, 1956), 22.

> of the service of those in whose company our lot is cast, that by the mouths of children and babes in arms praise may be perfect. Let us invite them: "Sing praises to God, sing praises!" And let us hear them in turn responding: "Sing praises to our king, sing praises!" Joined therefore as you are in songs of praise with heaven's own singers, since you too are citizens like all the saints, and part of God's household, sing wisely. As food is sweet to the palate, so does a psalm delight the heart. But the soul that is sincere and wise will not fail to chew the psalm with the teeth, as it were, of the mind, because if he swallows it in a lump, without proper mastication, the palate will be cheated of the delicious flavor, sweeter than honey that drips from the comb.[4]

Bernard advises another prayer as well, one which is also an ancient tradition: the frequent invocation of the name of Jesus in the heart. It strikes me that few things reveal Bernard more as Bernard than his references to the name of Jesus and the sheer joy that this name evokes in him:

> What other name can so enrich the man who meditates? What can equal its power to refresh the harassed senses, to buttress the virtues, to add vigor to good and upright habits, to foster chaste affections? Every food of the mind is dry if not dipped in that oil; it is tasteless if not seasoned by that salt. . . . Jesus to me is honey in the mouth, music in the ear, a song in the heart.[5]

As a companion to this practice, Bernard also invites us to invoke the name of Mary frequently:

> "And the Virgin's name was Mary." Let us now say a few words about this name. . . . In dangers, in hardships, in every doubt, think of Mary, call out to Mary. Keep her in your mouth, keep her in your heart. . . . With her leading you, you will never tire. Her kindness will see you through to the end. Then you

4. *SC*, CF 4:40–42.
5. *SC*, CF 4:110.

> will know by your own experience how true it is that "the Virgin's name was Mary."[6]

What is the mysterious power in this prayer of invocation? One hermit day in the woods, long ago, I discovered it and can never recall it without gratitude. In a time of great stress, I turned to Mary and called for hours upon her name, of whom Bernard says, "In her there is nothing austere."[7] The healing that came that day came through the experience of her presence. To call upon the names of Jesus and Mary in faith is to enter into the presence of Jesus, into the presence of Mary, it is to experience them. During a homily Dom Augustine Roberts once asked our community, "What is the particular devotion of Cistercians to Mary?" It is obviously not any of the many formulaic Marian devotions we Cistercians predate, founded as we were at the end of the eleventh century. Dom Augustine went on to say that it is simply *the experience of Mary,* and, it seems to me, that is what Bernard urges us to when he exhorts us to call upon her name.

The prayers, then—whether they be the psalms, invocations of the names of Jesus and Mary, or other heartfelt cries—draw our minds ever more fully toward the divine, and, by freeing us from compulsive ways of thinking, help us to be simply ourselves before God.

6. *Homilia super 'Missus est' in laudibus Virginis Matris, Magnificat,* CF 18 (Kalamazoo, MI: Cistercian Publications, 1979), 30–31.

7. *Sermo in octava Assumptionis B.V.M.,* in *Sermons for the Seasons and Principal Feasts of the Year,* 3:259.

Let us cry out, therefore,
with a voice that comes more
from the heart than from the lips:
"Save us, O Lord, our God,
and gather us from among the pagans,
that we may praise your holy name rather than our own,
and find our happiness in praising you instead of ourselves,
for ever and ever."[8]

8. *SC*, CF 4:96.

10

Works and Prayer: *Pietas*

The fourth infusion, *pietatis opus*, or "works motivated by love"—most especially that work of loving obedience to the Father which so fed the interior life of Jesus—is "a sure source of strength for us" as we keep vigil. The second stage is the time for growing in virtue, for going "from strength to strength" as the psalmist says (Ps 84:7), and this means, ultimately, becoming more and more like Jesus in our thoughts, words, and deeds. It is to be infused with his loving-kindness.

Loving-kindness or tenderness, in Latin *pietas*, expresses a very deep and full level of love in the thought of Saint Bernard, the love revealed in the heart of Christ on the cross. Again we turn to the passage from *Sermon 61* on the Song of Songs:

> The iron pierced his soul and his heart has drawn near, so that he is no longer one who cannot sympathize with my weaknesses. The secret of his heart is laid open through the clefts of his body; that mighty mystery of loving [*pietas*] is laid open, laid open to the tender mercies of our God, in which the morning sun from on high has risen upon us. Surely his heart is laid open through his wounds! Where more clearly than in your wounds does the evidence shine that you, Lord, "are good and forgiving, abounding in steadfast love"?[1]

1. *SC*, CF 31:144.

Likewise, *pietas* is the third and highest ointment, far excelling both compunction and devotion:

> But there is another ointment, far excelling these two, to which I give the name loving-kindness *(pietas),* because the elements that go to its making are the needs of the poor, the anxieties of the oppressed, the worries of those who are sad, the sins of wrong-doers, and finally, the manifold misfortunes of people of all classes who endure affliction, even if they are our enemies. These elements may seem rather depressing, but the ointment made from them is more fragrant than all other spices. It bears the power to heal, for "Happy are the merciful; they shall have mercy shown them." A collection therefore of manifold miseries on which the eye rests with loving-kindness represents the ingredients from which the best ointments are made.[2]

The works of loving service to others and the work of prayer are meant to become so integrated in a person that they resemble a seamless garment, one thing only; but naturally this integration takes time and presents us with many challenges. How to work in a prayerful way? How to avoid work that is an escape from prayer? How to avoid prayer that is an escape from others? How to know the difference? In this area we surely learn more from people than from books.

I have a sister who shines with this grace of *pietatis opus,* that is, with a deep integration of loving service and prayer. She is the first person one thinks of when a favor is needed, especially a humble one, because she will never say "no," and not only that, she will always say "yes" as if you were doing *her* a favor. And no, this sister is not in her first fervor. She has been in this mode for over thirty years! At the same time, she is a person deeply drawn to prayer and obviously absorbed in God no matter what she is doing. What is her secret? I often wondered. Then one day she shared with me an experience that gave me a light into God's mysterious ways. At the time several of the sisters took turns helping with the wheelchair transport of one of our dear elderly

2. *SC,* CF 4:77.

sisters who wanted to be present with the community for absolutely everything. If for some reason you couldn't make your assigned slot, you asked another to fill in. Of course, you can imagine that the sister I have been describing was often asked to do this at the last moment, given her approachability. One evening she was walking toward the church with an unusually acute longing to rest in God's presence at the end of a busy day when suddenly she heard, "Please, will you take Sister Stephanie back to her room for me?" At once, Sister felt the pain in her soul sharply, yet she responded with her accustomed "yes" to the gift of the moment. With great amazement she told me that, as she was preparing Sister Stephanie for bed, she was overcome with God's presence, a presence of such ineffable sweetness that it lingered through the night. How could she have deserved such a thing? I didn't answer, but my own question had been answered.

No doors are barred to God. In the midst of our labors he comes, filling them with himself, integrating all our scattered efforts, granting us interior rest. What also became clear to me is that the depth of our prayer life can best be measured by our loving-kindness toward others:

> And you too, if you will permit us your companions to share in the gift you have received from above, if you are at all times courteous, friendly, agreeable, gentle and humble, you will find men everywhere bearing witness to the perfumed influence you radiate. Everyone among you who not only patiently endures the bodily and mental weaknesses of his neighbors, but, if permissible and possible, even plies them with attentions, inspires them with encouragement, helps them with advice, or where the rules do not so permit, at least does not cease to assist them by fervent prayers—everyone, I repeat, who performs such deeds among you, gives forth a good odor among the brethren like a rare and delicate perfume. As balsam in the mouth, so is such a man in the community; people will point him out and say: "This is a man who loves his brothers and the people of Israel; this is a man who prays much for the people and for the holy city."[3]

3. *SC*, CF 4:81–82.

11

Interior Solitude

Finally we come to the fifth infusion, *orationis studium*, "eagerness for prayer."[1] We have seen how intimate is the converse into which God wishes to lead us, and we have seen also how the journey moves ever more deeply into the interior. "Within" *(intus)* is an important word for Bernard, for this is where God meets us. He looks for us in the secret places of our being that we are beginning to discover as we journey from the surface to the interior, as we take the path to the heart.

In *Sermon 31* Bernard has a careful development of this interior meeting, the deepest of three ways of seeing God. The first way, available to all, is the contemplation of creation in all its variety. All creatures are rays emanating from the Godhead, "showing that he from whom they come truly is, but not fully explaining what he is." The second is available to the few and consists of a "sweet communion with God who became present to them" by means of dreams, exterior visions, or words. But it is the third for which we were all created and toward which we journey day by day; "it takes place in the interior, when God is pleased to visit the soul that seeks him, provided it is committed to seeking him with all its desire and love."[2]

1. *SC*, CF 4:139.
2. *SC*, CF 7:127.

Interiority is the very quality that distinguishes the human person from all other created things,[3] and Bernard's expression of this truth is profoundly beautiful:

> One who is so disposed and so beloved will by no means be content either with that manifestation of the Bridegroom given to the many in the world of creatures or to the few in visions or dreams. By a special privilege she wants to welcome him down from heaven into her inmost heart, into her deepest love; she wants to have the one she desires present to her not in bodily form but by inward infusion, not by appearing externally but by laying hold of her within. It is beyond question that the vision is all the more delightful the more inward it is, and not external.[4]

What is Bernard's thought on solitude in the Cistercian life, since all intimacy requires solitude? What is its place, what is its practice in a form of community life that has little physical solitude? Consider the similarities in the following texts:

> O holy soul, remain alone, so that you might keep yourself for him alone whom you have chosen for yourself out of all that exist. . . . Can you not see how shy your Love is, that he will never come to you when others are present? Therefore you must withdraw, mentally rather than physically, in your intention, in your devotion, in your spirit. For Christ the Lord is a spirit before your face, and he demands solitude of the spirit more than of the body, although physical withdrawal can be of benefit when the opportunity offers, especially in the time of prayer. To do this is to follow the advice and example of the Bridegroom, that when you want to pray you should go into your room, shut the door and then pray. And what he said he did. He spent nights alone in prayer, not merely hiding from the crowds but even from his disciples and familiar friends. He did indeed take three of his friends with him when the hour of his

3. See Karol Wojtyła, *Love and Responsibility* (New York: Farrar, Straus & Giroux, 1982), 22–24.
4. *SC*, CF 7:129.

death was approaching; but the urge to pray drew him apart even from them.

You too must act like this when you wish to pray. Apart from that the only solitude prescribed for you is that of the mind and spirit. You enjoy this solitude if you refuse to share in the common gossip, if you shun involvement in the problems of the hour and set no store by the fancies that attract the masses; if you reject what everybody covets, avoid disputes, make light of losses, and pay no heed to injuries. Otherwise you are not alone even when alone. Do you not see that you can be alone when in company and in company when alone? However great the crowds that surround you, you can enjoy the benefits of solitude if you refrain from curiosity about other people's conduct and shun rash judgment.[5]

And from *Sermon 27* on the Song of Songs:

> What a capacity this soul has, how privileged its merits, that it is found worthy not only to receive the divine presence, but to be able to make sufficient room! What can I say of her who can provide avenues spacious enough for the God of majesty to walk in! She certainly cannot afford to be entangled in law-suits nor by worldly cares; she cannot be enslaved by gluttony and sensual pleasures, by the lust of the eyes, the ambition to rule, or by pride in the possession of power. If she is to become heaven, the dwelling-place of God, it is first of all essential that she be empty of all these defects. Otherwise how could she be still enough to know that he is God?[6]

These are words for all who take prayer seriously, active and contemplative alike. As Fr. Charles Dumont points out, Bernard's doctrine consistently unites the mystical and the ethical,[7] something so particularly clear in these passages. As we walk through our day there are choices to be made, and our avoidance of our evil inclinations leaves us alone with the Beloved, not in a way

5. *SC*, CF 7:202–3.
6. *SC*, CF 7:83.
7. See Dumont, *Pathway of Peace*, CS 187:210, 226.

that cuts us off from others, but in a way in which our lives flow from a center deeply grounded and fulfilled in the love that alone can satisfy.

In *Sermon 18* Bernard describes the infusion of prayer *(oratio,* not yet *contemplatio)* in a way that is similarly connected to the way we live:

> Food causes thirst, therefore one must drink, so let the food of good works be moistened with the beverage of prayer, that a work well done may rest quietly in the stomach of conscience and give pleasure to God. In prayer one drinks the wine that gladdens a man's heart, the intoxicating wine of the Spirit that drowns all memory of the pleasures of the flesh. It drenches anew the arid recesses of the conscience, stimulates digestion of the meats of good works, fills the faculties of the soul with a robust faith, a solid hope, a love that is living and true; it enriches all the actions of our life.[8]

One of the members of our lay group has her own way of leading her young fifth- and sixth-grade students into this experience, without even mentioning the word prayer. In the middle of her classroom, set up to foster the greatest possible connectedness between teacher and student and among the students themselves, there stands a solitary and lovely carrel named "Cîteaux." That is the place one goes to spend time alone and rest, a place to be still, a place to be renewed. It is an experience lived, not a theory taught, and on a deep level it is readily understood. Neither a way to escape others nor a punishment for hurting others, it becomes another way of experiencing communion. Sometimes even seventh- or eighth-graders ask if they can come back to Cîteaux for a while! Deep down we all move toward the truth that, when God alone is our center and when all our loves are ordered around him, then all our loves are true.

8. *SC*, 4:137–38.

O true noontide,
fullness of warmth and light,
trysting place of the sun;
noontide that blots out shadows, that dries up marshes,
that banishes evil odors!
O perpetual solstice,
with your spring-time freshness, your summer-like gracefulness,
your autumnal fruitfulness and—let me not seem to omit it—
your winter quiescence and leisure!
Show me this place where there is so much
brightness and peace and fullness.[9]

9. *SC*, CF 7:149–50.

12

Knowing Jesus

When considering the first stage of prayer, we looked at the Lord's tremendous pedagogy in meeting us on the level of human affection, our natural habitat, and drawing us to himself by his humanity. Prayer at this stage is naturally more affective as we experience the One who desires to accompany us in all our joys and sorrows and who knows from the inside what we experience. The Gospels, in particular, reveal to us one who is like us in all things except sin. It seems that the second stage of prayer, as I have considered it in Saint Bernard, is a continuation and development of the affective knowledge which began in the first. As we approach Jesus in the liturgy and in the Gospels day by day and year by year in order to open our lives to him, a wonderful bond begins to grow, a knitting together, an intimate companionship. Prayer here is the "wine that gladdens."[1]

This is not to say, however, that the experience is one of uninterrupted positive feeling. As mentioned earlier, God works by a process of alternating experiences to expand our hearts and to stretch us beyond our feelings and beyond ourselves:

> The Holy Spirit comes and goes, and if a man can stand firmly only with his support, it follows that he must fall when abandoned by him; fall, yes, but never fatally, since the Lord supports him by the hand. . . . Persons who are spiritual or whom

1. *SC*, CF 4:137.

> the Holy Spirit purposes to make spiritual, never cease to experience these alternations; he visits them every morning and tests them at any moment.[2]

What is this "falling" if not the darkness, the struggles, the waiting for the light that comprises so much of prayer's journey? But this too is an experience of God, an experience of his holiness, that is, his mysterious otherness. To live through these times faithfully is to grow in our capacity to receive God in all situations, for as our receptivity becomes less dependent on circumstances and feelings, an interior door opens up to another, deeper level. Bernard speaks of it as "knowing Christ spiritually," and in several sermons he contrasts the two ways of knowing him. In *Sermon 22* he does this by contrasting Christ's divine beauty with his human form:

> Far from disapproving of those whose purer mind enables them to grasp sublimer truths than I can present, I warmly congratulate them, but expect them to allow me to provide a simpler doctrine for simpler minds. How I wish that all had the gift of teaching: I should be rid of the need to preach these sermons! It is a burden I should like to transfer to another, or rather I should prefer that none of you would need to exercise it, that all would be taught by God, and I should have leisure to contemplate God's beauty. Now, however, I must confess, not without tears, that I have no time to seek after God, much less to contemplate him; no time to see the king in his beauty seated upon the Cherubim, on a throne raised aloft; to see him in that form in which, as the Father's equal, he was born before the dawning amid the sacred splendors. This is the form in which the angels long to contemplate him forever, God with God; and I, a man, describe him to men according to the human form that he adopted in order to reveal himself with the maximum of esteem and love. "Made lower than the angels," he came out of his chambers like a Bridegroom and pitched a tent in the sun. I present him as attractive rather than sublime.[3]

2. *SC*, CF 4:127.
3. *SC*, CF 7:15–16.

This divine beauty—how Bernard longed for it, an indication of how he must have been burned by it!

> She [the soul] therefore will touch me worthily who will accept me as seated with the Father, no longer in lowly guise, but in my own flesh transformed with heaven's beauty. . . . Become beautiful and then touch me; live by faith and you are beautiful. In your beauty you will touch my beauty all the more worthily, with greater felicity. You will touch me with the hand of faith, the finger of desire, the embrace of love; you will touch me with the mind's eye.[4]

And again:

> The bride speaks in her turn: "Behold, how beautiful you are, my love, how beautiful." . . . A tremendous vision indeed that endows her with such confidence and prestige that she greets this Lord of all things not as her lord but as her beloved. For I believe that in this vision images of his flesh, or of the cross, or in any way suggestive of physical frailty, were not imprinted on her imagination, since the Prophet tells us that under these forms he possessed neither beauty nor majesty. But as she now contemplates him, she declares him both beautiful and majestic, making it clear that her present vision transcended all others. He speaks to her face to face as once he spoke to Moses, and she for her part sees God plainly. . . . Her eyes beheld the king in his beauty, though to her he was not king but her beloved.[5]

Is such a vision for this earth? Clearly yes, though in a mirror darkly. And so we come to the sixth infusion, in which Bernard points out, as he often does, that the contemplative experience is rare and brief, yet powerfully transformative:

> The sick man has had his food and drink; what should he do now but take his ease and let the sweat of his labors dry while

4. *SC*, CF 7:96.
5. *SC*, CF 7:236–37.

> he enjoys the quiet of contemplation. Falling asleep in the midst of his prayer he dreams of God; what he sees is a dim reflection in a mirror, not a vision face to face. However, although it be but a vague apprehension and not an actual vision, a fleeting glimpse of the sparkling glory as it passes, utterly delicate in its impact, yet he burns with love and says: "At night my soul longs for you and my spirit in me seeks for you." A love like this is full of zeal; it is a love becoming the Bridegroom's friend.[6]

It is now time to explore this way of knowing Jesus, to consider Bernard's rich teaching on *contemplatio.* Although I am personally far from having experienced all that he speaks of, I will try to be true to the clues he gives for this third stage of prayer.

May he come down as from the mountains of Bethel, full of
joy and radiance,
descending from the Father, sweet and gentle,
not scorning to become and to be known
as the Bridegroom of the soul who seeks him,
for he is God, blessed above all forever.[7]

6. *SC*, CF 4:138.
7. *SC*, CF 40:96.

13

Crossing Over

How does one cross over to the third stage? How does one progress from a predominantly affective experience of God to what Bernard calls a spiritual one? Bernard doesn't speak of a bridge or even of a crossing over as far as I know, but he does describe clearly what needs to be in place before one advances interiorly.

In the three steps of truth he speaks of profound sympathy with the weaknesses of others as the disposition that clears the heart to see God. In the three kisses he presents another criterion for profound spiritual union: loving the truth as well as understanding it. In *Sermon 64,* in which he speaks of the temptations proper to each stage, he gives a glimpse of very definite and difficult choices proficients must make in the spiritual journey:

> Now there are different kinds of temptation, corresponding to different times [in our lives]. At the beginning of our course, when we are like tender flowers on young plants, a sharp frost attacks us openly. . . . Yet the powerful enemies of good do not dare openly to oppose the proficient, who have made some progress in sanctity, but they lie in wait for them in secret, like cunning little foxes, wearing the likeness of virtues, whereas they are really vices. How many, for instance, have I known who, at the beginning of life's journey, started out all right on the paths of righteousness and were making serene progress towards goodness when, for shame! they suffer the humiliation of being tripped up by these little foxes,

> and too late they grieve for the fruits of virtue which have been choked in them.[1]

Bernard then lists four possible temptations: to leave one's community and share one's precious lights and fruits with those to whom one is bound most closely; to leave and proclaim them from the housetops; to leave and enter into the depths of solitude as a hermit; or to remain and practice extreme austerity. What all these temptations have in common is nobility of goal—"that the strong have something to yearn for"[2]—and this nobility makes it difficult to see that these so-called inspirations are actually temptations. As Bernard points out, the mark of temptations in this stage is subtlety:

> Now let us consider what the Bridegroom said about these cunning little animals that spoil the vines. They are little, I would say, not because they have little malice, but because of their subtlety. This kind of creature is indeed cunning by nature, and exceedingly quick to do damage in secret, and it may, I think, be most appropriate to consider them as representing certain subtle vices cloaked in the likeness of virtues. . . . They can do no damage at all except by falsely representing themselves as virtues, because of their very likeness to virtues. For they are either the vain thoughts of men or the promptings of Satan's evil angels, who disguise themselves as angels of light, making ready their arrows in the quiver—that is, in secret—to shoot in the dark at the upright of heart. That, I think, is why they are called little, for while other vices show themselves as it were in bodily form, this kind are not easily recognized because of their subtlety. They cannot easily be avoided except by the perfect and the experienced, and by such as have the eyes of their souls enlightened for the discernment of good and evil, and particularly for the discernment of spirits.[3]

1. *SC*, CF 31:169–70.
2. Rule of Saint Benedict 1980, ed. Timothy Fry (Collegeville, MN: Liturgical Press, 1981), 64.19.
3. *SC*, CF 31:173–74.

Part of the subtlety must surely come from a sense of spiritual prosperity, for, as Bernard puts it in another passage when speaking of temptations: "Through the first stage of charity the ignorant person is initiated, through the second the initiate is encouraged forward, and through the third, already well advanced, he is firmly strengthened. . . . Adverse circumstances undermine the first kind of charity and prosperity carries off the second, but the third has been built upon a rock."[4]

What can we do, then, to avoid these temptations that seem to lead to the peak of spiritual fulfillment? One possibility is not to make any external change in our situation, while simply allowing desire to build up in the soul as water fills a reservoir. This isn't easy, because although the temptations are subtle, they are really stretching us to our limits; they are desires aiming to displace our central desire. On one level we want very much to remain prosperous and secure spiritually; that is, we want to continue *feeling* prosperous and secure. What we have known of God's ways in our lives so far, we have loved; but there is an unknown ahead, an unknown of God and an unknown of ourselves. Will we go forward or will we find every possible way to remain in our prosperity, which amounts to saying that we will cease to grow? Perhaps it is true, as I have often heard said, that many do stop growing at this point. Somehow enough is enough. Saint Francis de Sales lamented the fact that "one still sees too many who are content only with eating at the feast of love. A few dare to drink 'with pleasure and abundantly,' but so few go to the extent of getting drunk!"[5]

I like to imagine that Saint Bernard's temptation to stop growing may have been at his experience of the failure of the Second Crusade. Having reached such a pitch of glory and fervor in preaching it, it seems only reasonable that he would in some way want to vindicate himself. But his response reveals that even at this difficult moment he chose to put God before himself:

4. *Sent*, CF 55:303.

5. Blaise Arminjon, *The Cantata of Love* (San Francisco: Ignatius Press, 1988), 232.

> I prefer that the murmurings of men be against me rather than against God, if a choice must be made. What an honor for me if he deigns to use me for a shield. Willingly I draw to myself the scurrilous tongues of detractors and the poisoned darts of blasphemers so that they do not reach him. I do not refuse to be stripped of glory to prevent an attack on the glory of God. Who can enable me to glory in these words, "For you I have endured reproach; shame has covered my face"? For me, glory is to become a companion of Christ who said, "The reproaches of those who accuse you have fallen on me."[6]

Ultimately it comes down to the cross. If we can identify with Jesus in his passion and death no matter what befalls us, the cross itself will be the bridge by which we pass over to the other side.

> *Repentant sinners, therefore, who wish to attain to that holiness essential for the vision of God, should listen to your warning: "Be holy, for I am holy." Let them pay attention to your ways for you are just in all your ways and holy in all your doings. Finally, how many are inspired to run by the sweet odor of your redemption! When you are lifted up from the earth you draw all things to yourself. Your Passion is the ultimate refuge, a remedy that is unique. When our wisdom lets us down, when our righteousness falls short, when the merits of our holiness flounder, your Passion becomes our support. . . . When my strength is spent I shall not be troubled, I shall not lose heart. I know what I shall do: "I will lift up the cup of salvation and call on the name of the Lord."*[7]

6. *Csi*, CF 37:52.
7. *SC*, CF 7:20–21.

Stage Three

And now what remains, O good Jesus, except that, suffused as I am with the fullness of your light, and while my spirit is fervent, you would graciously bestow on me the kiss of your mouth, and give me unbounded joy in your presence.[1]

1. *SC*, CF 4:20.

14

Contemplatio/Quies

Finally we enter upon the stage that is least known both because it is the least experienced and also because, when experienced, it is the most secret—as secret as the "new name, which no one knows except the one who receives it" (Rev 2:17): "For he has more than one queen. . . . And each has her secret rendezvous with the Bridegroom and says: 'My secret to myself, my secret to myself.'"[1]

How, then, to speak about a secret? Taking Bernard's lead, let's consider the sixth infusion quoted above, for in it he describes how *oratio* passes into *contemplatio*, and he gives us as well significant words and phrases: "quiet of contemplation," "dim reflection in a mirror," "dreams of God," "fleeting glimpse of the sparkling glory . . . utterly delicate in its impact."[2] In conjunction with this I would like to consider a similar passage in which Bernard makes the distinction between *contemplatio* and *oratio* even clearer:

> The drinking which cheers the soul is prayer. One who wishes to be with God ought to pray frequently. For when we pray, we speak with God; and when we read meditatively, God speaks with us. . . . After food and drink, the patient is allowed rest and sleep so that he may recover fully. This signifies a taste of

1. *SC*, CF 7:34.
2. *SC*, CF 4:138.

> contemplation, through which there is silence in heaven for about half an hour—that is, peace and the freedom of blessed tranquility in the soul of the just. For Christ sometimes visits the soul through contemplation—not in such a way as to instill himself totally in it, but so as to offer a taste of himself—not to fulfill the soul's desire, but rather to prolong her love. He grants certain first-fruits of his love, without bestowing the richness of complete fulfillment. . . . For the present he discloses from time to time, through a slight taste and a kind of foreshadowing, how truly blessed is the saints' expectation of his glory and sweetness. By reason of this gift of contemplation, the Spirit is said to be our tranquility, for it is written: "You will find rest for your souls."[3]

The images here involve taste, not sight, but the message is the same: prayer is conversation with God, heartfelt and frequent; contemplation is rest in God, quiet and less frequent. The one distinct element in the second passage is the mention of Christ who visits the soul, not in such a way as to instill himself totally in it, a thought we will return to later. For now, though, let's look at the most striking common elements—quiet, silence, delicacy, peace, rest. This is the spirituality of *quies*, in Greek *hesychia*, which so imbued our founding fathers that they described the way of living the Cistercian life as *conquiescere*: living together in *quies*. It is a way of prayer and, more particularly, a stage of prayer, the stage when the passions are quieted, words few, the heart intently still as it waits for his knock at the door. "Silence in heaven for half an hour" is a most apt biblical image for it, an image Bernard uses also in the third stage of truth, for it points both to the interior silence that is characteristic of this stage and to the brevity of contemplative experience. We receive glimpses and tastes only, and then we return to an abiding readiness to open the door if and when he should return.

What sort of shift occurs in the affect at this stage? Beyond the fact that the passions are quieter and the heart, after years of turn-

3. *Sent*, CF 55:97.

ing to the Lord, is more grounded in attentiveness, what is the precise difference between knowing Jesus affectively and knowing him spiritually? I think Bernard tries to give an answer in the fourth step of love, tries to put into words something he has tasted:

> When will this sort of affection be felt that, inebriated with divine love, the mind may forget itself? . . . To lose yourself, as if you no longer existed, to cease completely to experience yourself, to reduce yourself to nothing, is not a human sentiment but a divine experience. . . . It is necessary for the saints that all human feelings melt in a mysterious way and flow into the will of God. Otherwise, how will God be all in all?[4]

We are dealing here with a self-forgetfulness not only on the level of thought and choice, but also on the level of feeling, at least sometimes. This is a very extensive transformation of the person. Once in a while I get a glimpse of it when speaking with an older sister of our monastery whom everyone recognizes as being completely herself. Our dialogue might go something like this:

> "How are you? How is prayer?"
> "I'm just there. Nothing happens."
> "Are you sure?"
> "Yes."
> "Could you live without it?"
> "Oh no!"
> "What do you most desire?"
> "I want God. In darkness."

In darkness. This is not an image Bernard pursues, but I believe he is saying something very similar when he touches upon the mystery of human feelings no longer conscious of themselves because they are so intent on the Other.

4. *Dil*, CF 13B:119–20.

"Who will climb the mountain of the Lord?" "Who will give me the wings of a dove, that I may fly away to find rest?" This place is made peaceful, a dwelling-place in Sion. Alas for me, my exile has been lengthened. When will flesh and blood, this vessel of clay, this earthly dwelling, understand the fact? When will this sort of affection be felt that, inebriated with divine love, the mind may forget itself and become in its own eyes like a broken dish, hastening after God and clinging to him, becoming one with him in spirit, saying: "My flesh and my heart have wasted away. O God of my heart, O God, my share for eternity."[5]

5. *Dil,* CF 13B:119.

15

The Word: We Have Seen His Glory

As we enter more deeply into Saint Bernard's thought on contemplation, we may notice a marked shift in the title he gives Jesus in his later *Sermons on the Song of Songs*: the Word. With John the Evangelist, the contemplative soul "may enter into the inward being of the Word by the energy and purity of his mind."[1] In the following texts we see again the contrast between knowing Jesus affectively and knowing him spiritually:

> Happy the mind which frequently works at hollowing a place for itself in the wall, but happier still the one which does so in the rock! . . . But for this the mind must have a keener edge, a more eager purpose, and merits of a higher order. "Who is equal to such a calling?" Evidently he was who said: "In the beginning was the Word, and the Word was with God, and the Word was God. He was in the beginning with God." Does it not seem to you that he had immersed himself in the very inward being of the Word, and from the hidden recesses of his breast had drawn forth the holiest essence of divine wisdom?[2]
>
> The Church as a whole cannot draw near to make clefts in the rock—for it is not within the power of everybody in the Church to examine the mysteries of the divine will or of themselves to pierce the depths of God—therefore she is shown to dwell not only in the clefts of the rock but also in the crannies of the wall.

1. *SC*, CF 31:158.
2. *SC*, CF 31:152–53.

> Accordingly she dwells in the clefts of the rock through her perfect [members] who by their purity of conscience dare to explore and penetrate into the secrets of wisdom, and can achieve this by their keenness of mind. As for the crannies of the wall, those who of themselves are unable or will not presume to dig in the rock, let them dig in the wall, content to gaze mentally upon the glory of the saints. If even this is not possible to someone, let him place before him Jesus and him crucified. . . . To the soul who is still weak and sluggish there is shown a hollow in the ground where he may hide until he grows strong and vigorous enough to hollow out for himself clefts in the rock through which he may enter into the inward being of the Word by the energy and purity of his mind. . . . But when by dwelling in the hollow in the ground he will so have succeeded in healing his inward vision that he can gaze on the glory of God with unveiled face, . . . then at last, pleasing in both voice and face, he will confidently proclaim what he sees. [3]

Two times here Bernard speaks of entering into the inward being of the Word. How to describe such an experience? Think of the Christmas gospels: the Gospel of Luke at Midnight Mass with its delightfully concrete details of the child; the Prologue of John at the Day Mass, so full of awe before the Word who was with God, the Word who was God. It seems likely that every believing heart that truly listens to the Prologue feels itself drawn into the silence of heaven if but for a moment, feels its heart offered a fleeting glimpse of the Word's glory and a slight taste of his presence. If you know this experience, then you too can have some understanding of the heart that abides continually in quiet receptivity to the Word.

In Gregory of Nyssa's *Life of Moses* there is a passage with both similarities and a striking difference to those cited above, and since Bernard was influenced by Gregory's thought on image and likeness, it is possible that he also knew this text. What is similar is the movement toward contemplation, toward the inner being of God, with John the Evangelist as model. What differs is the

3. *SC*, CF 31:157–58.

marked way in which Gregory moves toward darkness and Bernard toward light:

> Scripture teaches by this that religious knowledge comes at first to those who receive it as light. Therefore what is perceived to be contrary to religion is darkness, and the escape from darkness comes about when one participates in light. But as the mind progresses and, through an ever greater and more perfect diligence, comes to apprehend reality, as it approaches more nearly to contemplation, it sees more clearly what of the divine nature is uncontemplated. For leaving behind everything that is observed, not only what sense comprehends but also what the intelligence thinks it sees, it keeps on penetrating deeper until by the intelligence's yearning for understanding it gains access to the invisible and the incomprehensible, and there it sees God. This is the true knowledge of what is sought; this is the seeing that consists in not seeing, because that which is sought transcends all knowledge, being separated on all sides by incomprehensibility as by a kind of darkness. Wherefore John the sublime, who penetrated into the luminous darkness, says, *No one has ever seen God*, thus asserting that knowledge of the divine essence is unattainable not only by men but also by every intelligent creature.[4]

I am not knowledgeable enough in the apophatic and kataphatic ways to make an in-depth comparison between Gregory's and Bernard's approaches, but one thing seems clear. Bernard moves unswervingly toward the light, running after the mystic who most inspired him and whom he puts on an equal footing with John in his initiation into heavenly mysteries: Saint Paul. In *Sermon 62*, when he speaks of John entering the inward being of the Word, he immediately continues: "What about him who imparted wisdom to the perfect, a wisdom wrapt in mystery, which none of the rulers of this age understood? Passing through the first and second heavens by his keen but holy curiosity, did the devout scrutinizer not gain at last this wisdom from the third?"[5] Certain

4. Gregory of Nyssa, *Life of Moses* (New York: Paulist Press, 1978), 95.
5. *SC*, CF 31:153.

words of Paul so influenced Bernard's description of contemplation (or, it might be more accurate to say, so clearly expressed what Bernard experienced) that he returns to them again and again. They are words that speak of light and vision—obscure light and partial vision, yes, but always the light:[6] "For now we see in a mirror, dimly, but then we will see face to face. Now I know only in part; then I will know fully, even as I have been fully known" (1 Cor 13:12). "When one turns to the Lord the veil is removed. . . . And all of us with unveiled faces, seeing the glory of the Lord as though reflected in a mirror, are being transformed into the same image from one degree of glory to another; for this comes from the Lord, the Spirit" (2 Cor 3:18).

And so, rather than speaking of a "luminous darkness," Bernard describes the inward vision as "gazing on the glory of God with unveiled face,"[7] a more truly Bernardine—and Pauline—description of what happens when one penetrates to the interior of the Word.

What does this mean for us today who are seeking to live Cistercian spirituality—or at least seeking to understand it? Personally, I think it has something—perhaps a great deal—to do with our Benedictine roots. In the first place, Benedict's emphasis on liturgical prayer immerses the monk in a very focused way in the paschal mystery, a mystery in which one experiences continually the movement from death to life and from darkness to light. By means of the recurring cycles of the liturgical year, one is always moving toward the light, hopefully at ever deeper levels. Secondly, the Benedictine spirit of poverty also moves toward the light. In his chapter on poverty in *Benedictine Monachism,* Dom Cuthbert Butler states: "Benedictines have never had any scruple about the

6. See "Introduction to Guerric of Igny," by John Morson and Hilary Costello, in Guerric of Igny, *Liturgical Sermons,* CF 8 (Spencer: Cistercian Publications, 1971), xli. They here state that the characteristic Cistercian theology is "a theology of light rather than of darkness. Although we are told repeatedly that man's knowledge of God in this life is as 'in a mirror dimly' still the statement is by way of affirmation."

7. *SC,* CF 31:158.

three elementary luxuries, light, space, air."[8] If any followers of Saint Benedict ever exemplified this totally, it is the Cistercians, as can be seen in their architecture, stripped of everything but the play of shadow and light; in their work, so often close to earth and sky; in their enclosure, formed by the rural space about them rather than grilles; in their emphasis on simplicity and on cultivating "an uncomplicated relationship with the God of simplicity."[9]

Yes, that is our way, both materially and spiritually, and such a way tends toward being at home in our Father's house, being delighted with the experience of him whenever and wherever it should come, being hungry for the light and eager to taste and touch and hear and see with those interior senses so strong in the Fathers of the Church and in Saint Benedict as well. I can only urge you not to be afraid when you find the same longings, the same eagerness in your heart. Go forward. God will take care of the interior purifications, the dark nights, in his time and way; but when he passes before you fleetingly in the glory he reveals in Jesus, do be there on the mountaintop to behold him. Let us be among those who cry, "We have seen his glory!"

> *Show me this place . . . where there is so much brightness and peace and fullness, so that, just as Jacob while still in this life saw the Lord face to face and his soul was saved; or as Moses saw him, not by means of images and obscure sayings or through dreams like some other prophets, but in a manner unrivalled and beyond the experience of all others, known only to himself and God; or as Isaiah, after the eyes of his heart had been opened, saw him seated on a high and exalted throne; or just as Paul, rapt into Paradise, heard words that he could not*

8. Cuthbert Butler, *Benedictine Monachism* (New York: Barnes & Noble, 1924), 157.

9. *Constitutions and Statutes of the Monks and Nuns of the Cistercian Order of the Strict Observance,* Constitution 27 (Rome: privately printed, 1990).

explain and saw his Lord Jesus Christ: so may I too merit the ecstatic grace of contemplating you in your light and beauty, as you generously feed your flock and make them rest securely.[10]

10. *SC*, CF 7:149–50.

16

One Spirit with Him

Although the creature loves less, being a lesser being, yet if it loves with its whole heart nothing is lacking, for it has given all. . . . Happy the soul who has been allowed to experience the embrace of such bliss! For it is nothing other than love, holy and chaste, full of sweetness and delight, love utterly serene and true, mutual and deep, which joins two beings, not in one flesh, but in one spirit, making them no longer two but one. As Paul says: "He who is united to God is one spirit with him."[1]

If there is one scriptural phrase that stands at the heart of Bernard's thought, a phrase omnipresent and theologically crucial, it is surely this one: "The one who adheres to the Lord is one spirit with him" (1 Cor 6:17). Michael Casey comments most lucidly on this passage:

> It must be said [that] the embrace of the Word is fundamentally the experience of the full implications of being in harmony with the will of God. This is not to be understood in the sense of mere objective conformity with positive prescriptions and legitimate commands, but rather as having all one's sensitivities and instincts suffused with spiritual light so that God's gift of himself is not so much "out there," as within, moulding subjectivity. The text which sprang most readily to Bernard's mind in this respect was 1 Cor 6:17: "The one who adheres to God is one spirit with him." The goal of desire for God and the culmination both of nature and of human striving is this *unitas spiritus.*

1. *SC*, CF 40:186.

> 1 Cor 6:17 is one of the most significant texts in Bernard's spirituality and, in some way, it summarizes his whole approach. The one who achieves spiritual union with God, whether this be understood as the contemplative experience during the course of this present life or the final felicity of the next, is the one who makes the effort to remain close to him in the practical details of living. Such a view of spiritual progress is proper not only to Bernard. It is strongly characteristic of Western mysticism in general and Benedictine monachism in particular.
>
> The text from Corinthians is often used yoked with Ps 72:8—*mihi adhærere Deo bonum est*—and occasionally with that of Ps 62:9—*adhæsit anima mea post te*—with the idea of adhesion as the joining point. *Adhærere* is said to connote a voluntary, even moral, adhesion to God which is effectively expressed as much in everyday conduct as in affective desire. "Union with God can never be anything but the accord of two distinct wills, and therefore this union with God can be effected in no other way than by and through love."[2]

Every step of the journey is leading to the moment when God brings about in us such likeness to the Word, such conformity to him, that we are no longer two but one spirit with him. This is the ultimate test of prayer's authenticity and depth: hearts turned from self-centeredness to God, hearts becoming more and more like Jesus. Naturally this is not always, perhaps not even often, self-evident. As a novice, troubled by what I considered a poor and empty prayer life, I approached my abbess to find out what was wrong. Maybe I really wasn't meant to be a contemplative, I suggested. Her response was immediate: "We don't judge it that way; 'by their fruits you shall know them.' The proof of your prayer is in your life, in the way you are living it." I left both encouraged and genuinely surprised. Here I quote the following passage from *Sermon 74* at length because of its great significance in demonstrating this truth:

> I want to tell you of my own experience as I promised. . . . I admit that the Word has also come to me—I speak as a fool—

2. Michael Casey, *Athirst for God*, CS 77:200–201.

> and has come many times. But although he has come to me, I have never been conscious of the moment of his coming. I perceived his presence, I remembered afterwards that he had been with me; sometimes I had a presentiment that he would come, but I was never conscious of his coming or his going. And where he comes from when he visits my soul, and where he goes, and by what means he enters and goes out, I admit that I do not know even now: as John says: "You do not know where he comes from or where he goes." There is nothing strange in this, for of him was it said, "Your footsteps will not be known." . . . How then did he enter? Perhaps he did not enter because he does not come from outside. He is not one of the things which exist outside us. Yet he does not come from within me, for he is good, and I know that there is no good in me. I have ascended to the highest in me, and look! The Word is towering above that. In my curiosity I have descended to explore my lowest depths, yet I found him even deeper. If I looked outside myself, I saw him stretching beyond the furthest I could see; and if I looked within, he was yet further within. Then I knew the truth of what I had read, "In him we live and move and have our being." . . . You ask then how I knew he was present, when his ways can in no way be traced? He is life and power, and as soon as he enters in, he awakens my slumbering soul; he stirs and soothes and pierces my heart, for before it was hard as stone, and diseased. . . . I knew the power of his might because my faults were put to flight and my human yearnings brought into subjection. I have marveled at the depth of his wisdom when my secret faults have been revealed and made visible; at the very slightest amendment of my way of life I have experienced his goodness and mercy; in the renewal and remaking of the spirit of my mind, that is of my inmost being, I have perceived the excellence of his glorious beauty.[3]

And so, in the end, prayer and love are one. Prayer opens us and conforms us more and more to the God who is love by disclosing to us the things in our heart that block love. Then, finally, one begins to approach the seventh infusion—love in all its fullness:

3. *SC*, CF 40:89–91.

> "At night my soul longs for you and my spirit in me seeks for you." A love like this is full of zeal, . . . a total love is the law in all its fullness, it can effectively fill the heart's capacity. Finally God himself is love, and nothing created can satisfy the man who is made to the image of God, except the God who is love, who alone is above all created natures.[4]

Perhaps the most beautiful example Bernard gives of the perfect integration of prayer and love in a concrete person can be found in his words to Gerard, his beloved and recently deceased brother, a brother whose life was filled with unselfish love expressed in service, and whose death was filled with ecstatic prayer:

> It is possible that, though you once knew us according to the flesh, you now no longer know us, and because you have entered into the power of the Lord you will be mindful of his righteousness alone, forgetful of ours. Furthermore, "he who is united to the Lord becomes one spirit with him," his whole being somehow changed into a movement of divine love. He no longer has the power to experience or relish anything but God and what God himself experiences and relishes, because he is filled with God. But God is love, and the deeper one's union with God, the more full one is of love. And though God cannot endure pain, he is not without compassion for those who do; it is his nature to show mercy and pardon. Therefore you too must of necessity be merciful, clasped as you are to him who is Mercy.[5]

To grow in prayer is to grow in love. To grow in love is to grow in prayer.

God is love,
and the deeper one's union with God,
the more full one is of love.[6]

4. *SC*, CF 4:138.
5. *SC*, CF 7:63.
6. Ibid.

17

The Mysticism of Obedience

If our goal is union with the Word, conformity to him, then obedience has from the start a mystical thrust in Cistercian spirituality. Again Michael Casey says it so well:

> In describing spiritual marriage, Bernard is speaking not about states of fervent elevation or about experiences as much as about the concord of wills which can be achieved only when the human being subjugates his will to that of his Creator. It is really a very humble event, with little of the spectacular about it. It is simply a matter of a little human being saying "Yes" to the mysterious power of divine love and allowing it to carry him beyond the narrowness of human perspectives into the boundlessness of God. Hence, it must be said, the embrace of the Word is fundamentally the experience of the full implications of living in harmony with the will of God.[1]

Indeed, this "very humble event," this "yes," is the breakthrough into both the boundlessness of God and profound intimacy with him. Bernard sees an exact correspondence between obedience and prayer:

> For she said "our bed," and "the beams of our houses," and "our paneling," thus boldly uniting herself in ownership to one with whom she knows she is united in love. It is not so with

1. Michael Casey, *Athirst for God*, CS 77:200.

> one who has not yet renounced her own will. She lies down by herself, she dwells by herself. . . . "From your precepts I learn wisdom," said the Psalmist, that you may know that the grace of contemplation is never owed except to the commandments. Do not imagine that love of your own repose is to become an obstacle to the way of obedience and the traditions of the seniors. If so, the Bridegroom will not sleep in the same bed with you, especially if, instead of the flowers of obedience, you have bestrewn it with the hemlock and nettles of disobedience. Because of this he will not listen to your prayers. When you call he will not come. Nor will this great lover of obedience who preferred to die rather than disobey, put himself into the power of one who will not obey.[2]

In my discouragement with my prayer life as a novice, I once said to my novice director: "I'm afraid I'm going to be a Martha, not a Mary." She didn't reply immediately, but a few days later in class she spoke of obedience, describing it as the "yes" that continually opens the door to God, moment by moment, event by event. Then she added: "For those of you who are worried that you may never be the contemplative Mary, have no fear. The way into his presence is the obedience that truly seeks to do his will and to be open to him in everything." That word was one of the great and unfailing lights along my Cistercian path, confirmed again and again by my experience and expressed in an incomparable way in these words of André Louf:

> One cannot talk about prayer without also referring to obedience. . . . Obedience is a language and a sign. It also effects something in the one who obeys. It lays his life entirely open to the requirements of an Other and binds him fast to that Other. More, much more even than that. It can engender new life. By laying someone open to an Other, it alters him in the deepest sense of the word. It is a new life-style, whereby a person can detach himself more and more from his own constricted state, so as to be engrossed in the richness of an Other and to share

2. *SC*, CF 7:243–44.

> that richness with Him. . . . According to the Letter to the Hebrews, Jesus said on coming into the world: "You who wanted no sacrifice or oblation prepared a body for me. . . . God, here I am! I am coming to obey your will." For Jesus this is to be a very painful experience; for our redemption consists precisely in the fact that His obedience as God now assumes a human form in a body and in a psychology marked by sin. . . . This bloody confrontation with His Father's Will in His human body ran right through His prayer: "Not My will but Your Will be done!" Jesus fought that battle in constant prayer; and He was answered through and beyond death. His prayer could only be a cry for obedience, and His obedience was all that He could pray. Deep within Jesus, the Will of the Father was at one with His most fervent longing to pray. Jesus was Himself, in His most intimate relationship to His Father, in the very core of His being: obedience-in-prayer.[3]

This brings us to the great significance of the will in Saint Bernard's thought. In his anthropology the will is the most decisive faculty when it comes to growth in God and union with him. It is the faculty of freedom: "Only the will, then—since by reason of its innate freedom, it can be compelled by no force or necessity to dissent from itself, or to consent in any matter in spite of itself—makes a creature righteous or unrighteous, capable and deserving of happiness or of sorrow, insofar as it shall have consented to righteousness or unrighteousness."[4] Yet the consent of the will to God, leading to total self-surrender to him, is not the final word in Bernard's mysticism of obedience, for true obedience, which is relational, opens us to the mystery of *common will.* Marion Rissetto, commenting on Bernard's development of the sixth and seventh leprosies in his *Third Sermon for Easter,* summarizes as follows:

3. André Louf, *Teach Us To Pray* (Chicago: Franciscan Herald Press, 1975), 27–28.

4. *De gratia et libero arbitrio, Treatises III* (Kalamazoo, MI: Cistercian Publications, 1977), 61.

> Although we have one faculty of willing, it has two contradictory modes of acting: *voluntas propria*, or selfish will, and *voluntas communis*, or loving will. It is common will that is natural to us. Self-will is simply a perversion, a corruption of our natural freedom. Common will is a will in common with God and with others, that is, with those others who are one with his will; it is a will that seeks the glory of God and the benefit of others; it is a will towards God and others. Self-will, on the contrary, is exclusively our own, seeking as it does personal interest and private agendas. It stands alone.[5]

What is being described here is what, in our own day, Pope John Paul II has called the *spirituality of communion*, which "indicates above all the heart's contemplation of the mystery of the Trinity dwelling in us" and, flowing from that, a loving mutual yielding born of faith in the profound unity of the Mystical Body. A spirituality of communion or "common will" knows how to make room for our brothers and sisters, bearing each other's burdens and resisting "the selfish temptations which constantly beset us and provoke competition, careerism, distrust and jealousy."[6] Clearly our practice of obedience is meant to stretch us beyond ourselves to a common will, that is, to that mutual obedience filled with fervent love described by Saint Benedict in RB 72, to seeking together the will of the Father.

I remember being amazed one day when a woman in our lay group told me that for the first time she and her husband had not yet yielded to each other on a particular point. I asked how it was possible that it was the first time. Had they truly practiced a perfect obedience all these years? As she explained to me that they had always tried to yield to each other when a difference arose, I

5. Marion Rissetto, OCSO, "Lectures on Bernard's 3rd Sermon for Easter" (unpublished manuscript), 83. See *Thomas Merton on Saint Bernard*, CS 9 (Kalamazoo, MI: Cistercian Publications, 1980) and Étienne Gilson's *The Mystical Theology of St. Bernard*, CS 120 (Kalamazoo, MI: Cistercian Publications, 1990) for her background material.

6. John Paul II, Apostolic Letter *Novo Millennio Ineunte* (Boston: Pauline Books and Media, 2000), 57.

suddenly understood common will afresh—two people or many people bound together in Christ, knowing without doubt that God has a plan for them and so desirous to know it and to do his will that they search for it together, listening and responding to one another rather than each insisting on his or her preferences. By their common search for the will of God, they enter into communion in fulfilling his plan.

Obedience, then, is a very great thing when viewed in relation to its goal. It is the practice and the promise that commits us to a long process of transformation in availability, receptivity, unselfishness, connectedness, relatedness. The more complete it becomes, the more it moves beyond the thing that is willed: "Perfect obedience knows no law. It can be held within no limits. Not content with the narrow bonds of obligation, it spreads to the fullness of charity, carried by its generous will."[7] And again, obedience is good when motivated by love, but perfect "when the command is received in the spirit in which it is given,"[8] which is to say that our love is even fuller when, in our obedience, we seek to remain receptive and related to the other by seeking to know what he or she truly desires. Obedience is ordained to unity, to communion, and thus to contemplation in which conformity to Christ is one of the major elements.

> *I am ready and am not troubled, that I may keep your commandments: not for once, not merely in part, but always and absolutely my heart is ready, O God, my heart is ready, ready to rejoice or to suffer, without making the least resistance to whatsoever you shall ordain. It may be that I feel a particular and very eager desire for repose: nevertheless I refuse not to labor, if such be your good pleasure. As it shall be the will of*

7. *De præcepto et dispensatione*, *Treatises I*, CF 1 (Spencer: Cistercian Publications, 1970), 114.

8. *Pre*, CF 1:116–17.

God in heaven, so be it done. I long for rest, but I refuse not to labor: let your will be done. Amen.[9]

9. *Sermo in festivitate S. Martini,* in *Sermons for the Seasons and Principal Feasts of the Year,* 3:24.

18

Contemplative Fruitfulness

Two things remain, prayer and love, and the greatest of these is love. In his masterful study of divine love in the thought of Saint Bernard, Pacificus Delfgaauw, states:

> All the great Bernardine treatises touch on the same vision: contemplation—foretaste of heavenly blessedness. Would that, then, be Bernard's last word on charity here below? All through the *Song* (but already elsewhere), another conviction emerges: true, chaste contemplation has this characteristic: it inspires zeal for souls, so that one willingly, and with complete freedom, interrupts one's *otium* in order to serve one's brothers. This is the concept of the fruitfulness of the Word's spouse. For Saint Bernard, above contemplation there is *plenitudo dilectionis, caritas abundans* that overflows to one's neighbor. He sees in that both the connatural effect and the authentic sign of true contemplation: *hoc vera et casta contemplatio habet*.[1]

In the words of Bernard himself: "Charity never lacks what is her own, all that she needs for her own security. Not alone does she have it, she abounds with it. She wants this abundance for herself that she may share it with all; and she reserves enough for herself so that she disappoints nobody. For charity is perfect only when full."[2]

1. Pacificus Delfgaauw, *Saint Bernard, Maître de l'amour divin* (doctoral thesis, 1952, published privately), 195 (translation mine).
2. *SC*, CF 4:135.

Delfgaauw goes on to note that there are three groups of texts that play with the theme of prayer/fraternal charity.[3] The first of these compares the surpassing excellence of contemplation with the necessity of action. For myself, I have long noticed that when it comes to the theme of the discernment of God's will in Bernard and other Cistercian fathers, the text of Philippians 1:23-24 is highly significant, whether directly cited or simply alluded to: "My desire is to depart and be with Christ, for that is far better. But to remain in the flesh is more necessary on your account." "Far better," "more necessary": these are the key words that reveal the text's presence. How to integrate these two ways of loving? As Bernard teaches, have greater esteem for the more excellent and intend it; yield quickly to the more necessary and embrace it:

> There is no doubt that, in a mind that loves rightly, the love of God is valued more than love of men, and among men themselves the more perfect [is esteemed] more than the weaker, heaven more than earth, eternity more than the flesh. In well-regulated action, on the other hand, the opposite order frequently or even always prevails. For we are more strongly impelled toward, and more often occupied with, the welfare of our neighbor; we attend our weaker brothers with more exacting care; by human right and very necessity we concentrate more on peace on earth than on the glory of heaven; by worrying about temporal cares we are not permitted to think of eternal things; in attending almost continually to the ills of our body we lay aside the care of our soul; and finally, in accord with the saying of the Apostle, we invest our weaker members with greater honor, so fulfilling in a sense the word of the Lord: "the last shall be first and the first last." Who will doubt that in prayer a man is speaking with God? But how often, at the call of charity, we are drawn away, torn away, for the sake of those who need to speak to us or be helped! How often does dutiful repose yield dutifully to the uproar of business! How often is a book laid aside in good conscience that we may sweat at manual work! How often, for the sake of administering worldly affairs,

3. See Delfgaauw, 196–97.

> we very rightly omit even the solemn celebration of Masses! A preposterous order; but necessity knows no law. Love in action devises its own order, in accord with the command of the householder, beginning with the most recent; it is certainly dutiful and correct, without favoritism, swayed not by worldly values but by human needs.
>
> But not so affective love, since it always leads the ordering from the first. It is the wisdom by which all things are experienced as they are; as for example, the higher the nature the more perfect the love it evokes; the lower evokes less, the lowest nothing. The truth of love determines the previous order but by this order the love of truth lays claim to itself. Now true love is found in this, that those whose need is greater receive first; and again loving truth is evident if we maintain in our feelings the order it maintains in the reason.[4]

This theme of affective/effective love, as well as the discernment of how to love when, as Saint Bernard would put it, "setting love in order," is an extremely important one in the spiritual journey; but it does not yet touch upon what we call "contemplative fruitfulness." Delfgaauw notes a second group of texts that speaks more explicitly of the necessity of interrupting contemplation for the salvation of souls. "[Contemplation] invites the bridegroom to repose, for the better thing is to remain at ease and be with Christ; but necessity drives one forth to help those who are to be saved."[5] Philippians 1:23-24 is transparently operative here.

But it is a third group of texts which touches directly upon our theme: contemplative prayer is fruitful and it delights in its fruitfulness. Here the sense of necessity fades while delight and desire come to the fore—the desire of Christ within us which urges us on to care for others with the same love with which he loves us:

> You must acknowledge here those changes that I have previously and more than once explained to you concerning holy inactivity and essential action, how this life does not cater for

4. *SC*, CF 31:34–35.
5. Delfgaauw, 195.

> constant contemplation or prolonged leisure, since we are impelled by the more cogent and more immediate demands of work and duty. When the Bridegroom therefore perceives, as he always does, that the bride has taken her rest for some time on his bosom, he does not hesitate to entice her out again to what seems more serviceable. It is not that she is unwilling, or that he himself is doing what he had forbidden. But if the bride is enticed by the Bridegroom this is because she receives from him the desire by which she is enticed, the desire of good works, the desire to bring forth fruit for the Bridegroom, for to her the Bridegroom is life, and death gain.
>
> And that desire is vehement: it urges her not only to arise but to arise quickly, for we read: "Arise, make haste, and come." It is no small consolation to her that she hears "come" and not "go," knowing from this that she is being invited rather than sent, and that the Bridegroom will be coming with her. For what will she reckon difficult with him as her companion?[6]

And in another sermon we read:

> The heart of the Bridegroom has faith in her, knowing her to be faithful, for she has rejected all things as dross to gain him. He knows her to be like him of whom it was said: "He is a chosen vessel for me." Paul's soul indeed was like a tender mother and a faithful wife when he said: "My little children, with whom I travail in birth again, until Christ shall be formed in you."[7]

Of course, we are not speaking here of those momentary experiences of genuine fraternal love of which, hopefully, our life is full, but of a stage, a season in which the soul bears fruit with delight in the love of Christ while somehow remaining in his presence. "The Bridegroom will be coming with her" as she goes out to care for others. This is the grace of spiritual motherhood of which Paul speaks, and of which Jesus also speaks: "How often would I have gathered your children together as a hen gathers her brood under her wings" (Luke 13:34.). For Bernard this is the third ointment,

6. *SC*, CF 31:108.
7. *SC*, CF 40:209.

that of loving-kindness, which marks those who have received the gift of prayer from above. They are persons who—at all times courteous, friendly, agreeable, gentle, and humble—give attention, encouragement, and advice to others;[8] they are true mothers who encourage and sympathize without intermission;[9] they are the reservoirs who pour out their gifts upon others from their overflowing fullness;[10] so, too, they are the ones in whom was infused in the wine room the unique and exquisite lesson of the Holy Spirit: that of being drunk with the wine of charity even to contempt for one's good name, to forgetfulness of self and to indifference to self-interest.[11]

Most, if not all, of us will feel far from a stage of prayer such as this, and yet we are drawn to it irresistibly by the Spirit of the One who calls us both to abide in him and to love our brothers and sisters with the love with which he has loved us. To love without limits, for this we were made, and it is prayer that moves us steadily onward toward the finish. And as we journey we are not without consolation, living as we do in the communion of saints and, most particularly, in the presence of the one saint who, for Bernard and for us, embodies more than any other the meaning of contemplative fruitfulness:

> Blessed Virgin,
> if there be anyone
> who remembers having called upon
> your mercy in need
> and it was lacking,
> let him be silent. . . .
>
> For it was this
> which gained a cure for the whole world
> and obtained salvation for every person.

8. See *SC*, CF 4:81.
9. See *SC*, CF 4:63.
10. See *SC*, CF 4:136.
11. See *SC*, CF 7:32.

For everyone knew
that you represented the entire human race
when you were told
Do not be afraid, Mary,
for you have found grace
as you asked.

Who then can explore
the length and breadth
the height and depth
of your mercy,
O blessed one?

Its length reaches even to the day of judgment
to all those who call upon it.

Its breadth fills the whole earth
so that the whole earth is filled with your mercy.

Its height attains the restoration of the eternal city
and its depth gains redemption
for those who sit
in darkness and the shadow of death.

Through you
heaven is filled
hell is emptied
the ruins of the heavenly Jerusalem are rebuilt
and lost life is given to those who wait
in wretchedness.

The utterly powerful and sympathetic charity
both in its compassionate attachment
and its supportive achievement
is equally rich in both.

To this fount therefore
may our thirsting souls hasten.
To this mound of mercy
may our distress race with reverence.[12]

12. *Sermon Four for the Feast of the Assumption*, 8–9, CF 65 (Kalamazoo, MI: Cistercian Publications, 2003), 366–68.

Epilogue

Does it really happen this way? Yes and no. No, because each person's prayer is an uncharted course to God, a hidden manna, a secret. Yes, because the Spirit guides us through the wisdom of others who are in communion with us on our journey home, others who have gone ahead of us and who have allowed Jesus to have his way in them. It is they who can tell us about Jesus, the Way.

When I was eighteen it was difficult for me to feel compunction, inexperienced as I was. I once heard a very experienced abbess who had entered at a young age describe that time of her life in these words: "Compunction at seventeen? Who wants it? Who needs it!" At that early stage my prayer received its impetus from several profound unitive moments with God that would mark my entire life. Since I was not ready to be punctured with contrition, he punctured me with joy, then divine tenderness, and finally a solitude so great I had no way out and no clue how to speak of it. No one can see God and live. It is true: I saw him and died. Nothing could again satisfy me except that interior wilderness where life is simply God to me and I to God.

But these blessed experiences take place in human persons who, like myself, are discovering life, awaking to its pleasures, struggling with evil inclinations—pride, lust, ambition, envy, and so on—who are falling, rising, falling, returning, falling, being lifted up. By the time I entered the monastery at age twenty-eight, compunction and contrition were the work of the day if I were to move through my sinfulness into steadfast devotion to the Lord Jesus.

Our interior lives do not all begin and end in the same way, and, as has been brought out in this study, Jesus meets us where we are. But cycles of growth are inevitable, and within these cycles are landmarks experienced by all who are willing to pass through and not around them. Saint Bernard is one who passed through, and he offers us clear and practical guidance that flows from personal experience and that has not ceased to flow since his days among us as a brother, a father, and a friend.

May his words on prayer be joy and light to all who take them to heart.

Index